Muslims Ask, Christians Answer

Christian W. Troll, S.J.

Muslims Ask, Christians Answer

Translated from the German
by David Marshall

New City Press
Hyde Park, New York

Published in the United States by New City Press
202 Comforter Blvd., Hyde Park, NY 12538
www.newcitypress.com
© 2012 Christian W. Troll

Cover design by Leandro de Leon

    Library of Congress Cataloging-in-Publication Data:
Troll, Christian W., 1937-
  [Muslime fragen, Christen antworten. English]
  Muslims ask, Christians answer / Christian W. Troll.
      p. cm.
  Includes bibliographical references (p.   ).
  ISBN 978-1-56548-430-6 (pbk. : alk. paper)
  1. Islam--Relations--Christianity. 2. Christianity and other
religions--Islam. 3. Religious pluralism. I. Title.
  BP172.T76613 2012
  261.2'7--dc23
                           2011043070

Printed in the United States of America

Contents

Introduction

Meetings between individual Muslims and Christians and also between church and mosque congregations are taking place today in more and more parts of the world. Joint projects in education and relief; visits to mosques and churches; dialogues in Muslim-Christian societies; lectures; discussions about local politics, and so on: these all provide opportunities for Christians and Muslims to ask questions about each other's faith and practice.

But are we Christians in fact prepared to give an adequate, sensitive and respectful account of our own faith? Do we have at our disposal the necessary background knowledge of the specific faith perspective and religious sensibility of Muslims?

This short book is primarily addressed to Christians; it seeks both to provide them with information and also to prompt them to engage in further reflection and learning. It might offer a basis and a reference-point for Christian groups seeking to understand more accurately the questions put to them by Muslims about the Christian faith and way of life, and also wishing to prepare themselves to respond to such questions as honestly and sympathetically as possible.

Islam contains at its very core a questioning of central Christian claims and of the concepts which arise from them. Muslims, with the Qur'an and the whole Islamic tradition as their starting point, will therefore continually articulate this questioning. This is an essential part of the mission with which all believing Muslims know themselves to have been entrusted. The Qur'an challenges Muslims to call others to Islam and also sets forth the way in which an appropriate dialogue should proceed: 'Invite to the way of your Lord with wisdom and beautiful preaching; and argue with them in ways that are best and most gracious: for your Lord knows best who have strayed from his path, and who receive guidance.' (16:125)

May this material contribute to the enrichment of religious dialogue between Muslim and Christian believers based on better and more objective information; may it encourage the discovery of shared foundations for living together in solidarity and peace; and may it also prompt each one of us to persist in the faithful search for the light of ever greater truth.

Christian W Troll SJ
Hochschule Sankt Georgen, Frankfurt a. M.

Editorial Note

From 1974 onwards a group of Christians in Tunisia in North Africa met regularly with Professor Robert Caspar, M. Afr., for joint discussion of a sequence of questions about Christian faith and practice regularly raised by Muslims. The work carried out by this group issued in 13 little chapters, each consisting of four stages: (I) formulation of the questions on one of the main themes, as Muslims express these questions; (II) the perspectives underlying these questions, first in general terms and then in greater detail; (III) Christian theological perspectives on the relevant questions; and finally (IV) suggestions for the formulation of actual Christian answers to the Muslim questions. A small book consisting of these 13 chapters appeared first in French and shortly afterwards, lightly revised, in English, under the title *Trying to Answer Questions* (Rome, Pontifical Institute for Arabic and Islamic Studies [PISAI], 1989).

On my return to Germany in 1999, after many years of experience and study of Muslim civilizations and of work with Muslims in different parts of the Christian-Islamic world, it very soon became clear to me that a thorough revision of this book was called for. At the Catholic Academy in Berlin a circle of Catholic and Protestant Christians met more or less monthly for more than two years from 1999 to 2002; the members were all living in contact with Muslims, and therefore the subject of the book was of great practical interest to them. We deliberately preserved the book's basic structure but left out a chapter dealing with questions about the presence of Christians in an almost exclusively Muslim country such as Tunisia. The material was critically revised, adapted and in parts substantially re-written.

My thanks go particularly to the Revd Dr Ulrich Schröter, who played a key editorial and theological role in the whole process; and also to my colleague Erhard Kunz SJ, Professor of Dogmatic Theology here at Hochschule Sankt Georgen in Frankfurt, who made some substantial improvements to the Christian theological responses, in some places completely re-writing them. Robert Kemal Kaya from Linz in Austria prepared a Turkish translation of this book, which has been published in Istanbul (San Antuan, 2003, frequent reprints), but which has attracted particular attention through the homepage http://www.islamacevaplar.com. I am indebted to my old friend the Revd Dr David Marshall not only for having translated the book accurately from German into English but has also for enhancing the text at many points in terms both of style and content. The English version thus in some respects improves on the German original. Together with the German version http://www.antwortenanmuslime.com, the English version www.answers-to-muslims.com and versions in five further major languages (Indonesian, Russian, Spanish, Italian and French) offer the opportunity for further questions to be raised and responses to be suggested. I record here my heartfelt thanks to all those who, in groups or as individuals, have shared in this project.

Chapter 1

Scripture and the Word of God

I. Muslim Questions

▶ Why are there four Gospels, rather than just one? Which is the authentic Gospel?

▶ Don't the discrepancies between the Gospels demonstrate that they have been corrupted?

▶ How can the Bible be the Word of God when individual books bear the names of their authors (Isaiah, Matthew, Mark, etc)? At best, these authors could be 'transmitters' of the revelation sent down upon them.

▶ How can the authors of the biblical books be reliable 'transmitters' when they are not direct eye-witnesses of the events recorded and do not even stand in an uninterrupted chain of transmitters, as is the case with the recognized Islamic Traditions (Hadith)? For example, Luke never met Jesus and does not state the names of those from whom he received his information (Luke 1:1-4).

II. Muslim Perspectives

General

The fundamental point here is that Muslims judge the Gospels – as indeed the Bible as a whole – by the standard of the Qur'an.

Islam sees the Qur'an as the model and the criterion for every Scripture revealed by God. The Qur'an is the direct Word of God, revealed to the Prophet, who is neither more nor less than the conveyor of this Word. The text is unique and unchangeable; it is in no sense the result of human creativity.

The Qur'an is the criterion (*al-furqân*) of the truth. Every other Scripture must be measured against it. The Bible, including the Gospels, can only be treated as the Word of God where it is in harmony with the Qur'an. Those who have the Qur'an have no need to read the other Scriptures, which have all either been altered, so that they no longer correspond with the texts as they were originally revealed, or have at least been wrongly understood. So there is little interest among Muslims in reading the Bible, except out of a curiosity to discover the sources of the distinctive doctrines and practices of Christians. Such curiosity is anyway regarded with some suspicion among Muslims, as calling into question the clear truth of the Qur'an as the final revelation.

Detailed

1. There is only one eternal Scripture, the 'mother of the book' (*umm al-kitâb*, Qur'an 13:39; 43:4; cf. 3:7).[1] This is the very Word of God, immaculately protected on the 'preserved tablet' (*al-lauh al-mahfûz*, Qur'an 85:22). In the course of time this original Scripture was revealed to prophets raised up by God: to Moses in the form of the Torah (more or less identical with the Pentateuch); to David in the form of the Psalms (*Zabûr*); to Jesus in the form of the Gospel (*Injîl*) and finally to Muhammad in the form of the Arabic Qur'an. All these Scriptures were 'sent down', dictated by God to the prophets, whose duty it was to transmit them word for word, without any corruption.

2. Each of these Scriptures is an edition of the one eternal Scripture. They all contain one and the same message, emphasizing the warning: 'You should worship and serve the one and only true God and set no other beings alongside him.' Thus far the Scriptures of the Jews and Christians agree

2

with the Qur'an, which, as the final and perfect edition of the Word of God, given in Arabic, contains the essential truths of all revealed Scripture, expressed with unsurpassable clarity and stylistic beauty. Where there is disagreement between the Bible and the Qur'an, this arises from the fact that the Jews and the Christians did not preserve their respective Scriptures perfectly, but corrupted them (*harrafa, tahrîf*).

3. Muslim theologians and apologists point to various ways in which the Torah and the Gospel have been corrupted.

   ♦ The first five books of the Bible (the Pentateuch) cannot in their entirety be attributed to Moses. For example, the description of his death at Deuteronomy 34:5-8 must have been written by somebody other than Moses. The Bible contains further editorial additions of this kind.

   ♦ The New Testament Gospels are full of contradictions, in, for example, their accounts of the genealogies of Jesus, his arrival at Jerusalem and Peter's betrayal of Jesus. Furthermore, they were composed by four different writers, at least one of whom never met Jesus. They thus fail to meet the most fundamental of the requirements for reliable transmission, as expressed in the concept of '*mutawâtir*' hadith, which requires that the attestation of a saying or deed of the Prophet must go back via an unbroken chain of transmitters to the original witness.

   ♦ Christians acknowledge that a number of 'apocryphal gospels' were not accepted into the Canon. One of these must have been the true Gospel which agrees with the Qur'an. Many Muslims believe that the 'Gospel of Barnabas' is precisely this authentic Gospel.[2]

   ♦ It is well known that Christians have suppressed references to the coming of Muhammad in both the Torah and the Gospel (Qur'an 7:157; 61:6). Nevertheless, there are still traces of these predictions in the existing text of the Bible. The Torah speaks of a prophet 'like Moses' who is to come: 'The Lord your God will raise up for you

3

a prophet like me from among your own people; you shall heed such a prophet . . . " I will raise up for them a prophet like you from among their own people; I will put my words in the mouth of the prophet, who shall speak to them everything that I command"' (Deuteronomy 18:15,18)[3]. John's Gospel speaks of one who will come after Jesus and teach the disciples all truth (John 14:16,26; 15:26; 16:13).

♦ There are, however, some Muslims scholars, past and present,[4] who have accepted the text of the Bible as it stands today. They suggest that the corruption of which the Qur'an speaks refers to misguided interpretation of the text by Jews and Christians from earliest times rather than to alteration of the actual text. Other contemporary Muslim scholars[5] recognize that the Gospels are based on knowledge of historical events, but add that the Christian interpretation of these events need not exclude other (e.g. Muslim) interpretations of them.

♦ It should also be noted that some contemporary Muslim scholars[6] have begun to apply the principles of modern textual scholarship to the study of the Qur'an. They have, however, encountered considerable difficulties in their own societies, from both political and academic sources.

III. Christian Perspectives

1. For Christians, the 'word of God' is not in the first instance the written word of Scripture but rather the event to which Scripture bears witness, i.e., God's communication of himself in human history. The Old Testament bears witness to the Exodus as liberation from slavery in Egypt and presents the making of the Covenant on Sinai and the occupation of the Promised Land as expressing the purposes of God, who is and will be with his people to save them. Christians find expressed in the writings of the New Testament their faith that Jesus Christ, the Word of God, is the definitive and perfect revelation of the God of Israel for all people. Among the Gospels there are differences in selection and emphasis; this can be seen, for example, in a

comparison of the four passion-narratives. What is, however, common to all the traditions contained within the New Testament (i.e., Gospels, Acts of the Apostles, Letters, Revelation) is that they present the deeds and words of Jesus in the light of his Resurrection. It is above all the Resurrection of Jesus that reveals his true identity and the depths of his words.

2. The Bible, including the Gospels, was written by authors 'inspired' by God; it is the word of God insofar as it was written under divine inspiration. Many biblical books were written down after a period of oral transmission. The result is the collection of texts, identified and preserved by the Church, which we call the Bible, including both the 'Old' or 'First' Testament and the 'New' or 'Second' Testament. The Church believes that these Scriptures, taken together in their totality, bear witness to the action and self-revelation of God. As believers we therefore encounter here the word of God. Just as the apostles consistently pointed back to the Scriptures (i.e., the Old Testament, at that time), so we also, if we are to recognize the word of God in the whole Bible, must likewise attend carefully to the Old Testament.

3. The word of God comes to us in human language. When the prophets speak the word of God they do so with detailed reference to the settings which they are addressing and to the groups of disciples who gather around them. Likewise, the Gospels communicate their message into the varied contexts of different early Christian communities. This explains why there is diversity within both Old and New Testaments, reflecting diverse perspectives on the same revelation. The biblical authors do not merely pass on words dictated to them; rather, in the distinctive ways in which they express the word of God that they have received, they bear witness to the fact that that word is a living reality.

Modern textual analysis aims to establish what material in the Gospels can be ascribed directly to Jesus and what derives from the witness of the early communities. As we thus identify the essential principles of interpretation which were already at work within the Scriptures themselves, we will be helped to understand the significance of Jesus for our contemporary situation.

IV. Christian Answers

1. It is essential above all to grasp that the Muslim approach is to think of the Gospel in terms of the Qur'an, as a form or version of the Qur'an. Only then is it possible to speak meaningfully in dialogue with Muslims from the perspective of the Christian faith, based on the message of the Gospels.

2. It is not a helpful starting-point for dialogue to focus on the differences between the Gospels or (responding to the view that these differences are a 'problem') to present historical explanations for them. Instead, the *content* of the Gospels should be emphasized.

3. The Gospel is emphatically not a book. The Greek word *'euangelion'* means the 'Good News (of salvation)' (*al-bushra*). Its content is the message of the love of God, communicated by Jesus, the Son of God. This message was not initially written down but was proclaimed by Jesus and then – again orally, not in writing – was passed on by his disciples, who lived with him and became witnesses of his life, suffering, death and Resurrection.

4. We bear witness that Jesus himself is the Word of God, God's self-revelation. The Qur'an also calls Jesus 'Word of God' (*kalimat Allâh*, Qur'an 4:171; cf. 3:39-45), without, however, understanding Jesus as the Son of God.

5. With the four Gospels we arrive at written testimony about Jesus. They were written in the light of faith in Jesus as the Risen One and expect from the hearer or reader the same faith; they ask us whether we too will encounter Jesus as Lord.

6. The four Gospels embody the Tradition of the Church, the extension in scriptural form, in the believing community, of the message of Jesus. This was originally proclaimed orally and reached written form in the second half of the first century. This understanding of the Gospels is to some degree

analogous to the Muslim concept of *Sunna* – the preservation, outside the Qur'an, of traditions about Muhammad's words and deeds.

7. The earliest New Testament manuscripts date from the beginning of the 2nd century. As is the case with the Bible as a whole, ancient manuscripts of the Gospels contain a number of variant readings. There is substantial agreement between the different manuscripts but there are also some significant differences. By applying the methods of textual criticism it is possible to reconstruct the original text with some confidence. Critical editions of the biblical text have been published and these editions take into consideration the most significant textual variants. The early Christian writings (Gospels, Letters, etc.) were gathered together by the Church into the Canon. In this process the Church did not acknowledge all available writings as authentic; some were excluded from the Canon and came to be known as 'apocryphal'.

8. It is a non-negotiable basis for dialogue that each side should acknowledge that the Scripture on which the faith of the other community is founded forms the basis and the norm for the understanding and the expression of that faith. This point, which was recognized at the Muslim-Christian Congress held in Tripoli, Libya, in February 1976, also implies the importance of Christians studying the Qur'an and Muslims studying the Bible if the dialogue between them is to be meaningful.

9. Like any other historical document, the Bible can be studied from outside the assumptions of the Christian faith. Thus the Gospels have been interpreted from a variety of positions, producing, for example, rationalist, Marxist, Jewish and even Muslim readings of the events which the Gospels describe. Each such reading deserves respect insofar as it takes seriously the intention of the text itself. In keeping with this concern to respect the 'otherness' of texts, it is to be hoped that dialogue between Christians and Muslims will take seriously the differences between the Qur'an and the Bible.

Chapter 2

The Divinity of Jesus and the Incarnation

I. Muslim Questions

▸ Jesus is one of a long line of prophets. How can he be greater than Muhammad, who is the 'Seal of the Prophets'?

▸ Jesus ranks as a great prophet who was born in a miraculous way, without a father; he also performed great miracles. But does this justify making him into a God?

▸ How can a human being at the same time be God?

▸ How can God let his prophet die on the cross? How ought we to conceive of a God who suffers and dies?

II. Muslim Perspectives

General

The transcendence of God means that he is utterly different from everything that has been created. Muslims feel thoroughly horrified by every attempt to 'associate' with God anything from the created order (human beings included), to place it beside God (*shirk*) or to 'assimilate' it with God (*tashbîh*). This feeling of horror is entirely in harmony with the Qur'an, which condemns any such attempts repeatedly and vehemently.

Titles applied by Christians to Jesus (e.g., 'Son of God') and to Mary (e.g., 'Mother of God') sound blasphemous to Muslim ears.

Realistic portrayals of the crucified Jesus are offensive to Muslims since Islam rejects sculptures of human beings, and especially of prophets.

Detailed

The Qur'an often underlines the transcendence of God: 'There is nothing whatever like unto him' (42:11). He is the creator of all things and is radically different from everything in the created order.

In the long sequence of prophets an outstanding position is ascribed to Jesus.

'We gave him [Abraham] Isaac and Jacob: all of them we guided. And before him we guided Noah, and, among his offspring, David, Solomon, Job, Joseph, Moses and Aaron; thus do we reward those who do good. And Zechariah and John, and Jesus and Elijah, all in the ranks of the righteous. And Ishmael, and Elisha, and Jonah, and Lot; and to all we gave favour above the nations. And to their fathers and offspring and brethren; we chose them and we guided them to a straight way' (6:84-87).

'To Jesus, the son of Mary, we gave clear signs, and strengthened him with the holy spirit' (2:253).

Jesus, who had been proclaimed – literally 'confirmed' (Qur'an 3:39) - by John the Baptist, was born of the Virgin Mary, without a human father.

'Then we sent to her [Mary] our angel, and he appeared to her as a man in all respects. She said: "I seek refuge from you in Allah the most gracious . . . " He said: "I am only a messenger from your Lord to announce to you the gift of a holy son." She said: "How shall I have a son, seeing that no man has touched me, and I am not unchaste?" He said: "So it will be. Your Lord says: 'That is easy for me, and we appoint him as a sign unto men and a mercy from us.' It is a matter decreed." So she conceived him and she retired with him to a remote place' (19:17-22).

Jesus preached pure monotheism and performed great miracles. The Jews tried to crucify Jesus but God saved him by raising him to himself. Jesus will come again at the end of time as a sign that the end of the world and the day of judgement are imminent.

'Behold! Allah said: "O Jesus! I will take you and raise you to myself and clear you (of the falsehoods) of those who blaspheme; I will make those who follow you superior to those who reject faith, to the Day of Resurrection. Then shall you all return to me and I will judge between you in the matters over which you dispute" (3:55).

'That they said: "We killed Christ Jesus, the son of Mary, the messenger of Allah" – but they did not kill him, neither did they crucify him, but so it was made to appear to them. And those who differ about it are full of doubts, with no knowledge but only conjecture to follow. They certainly did not kill him – no, Allah raised him up unto himself; and Allah is exalted in power, wise' (4:157-158).

[The infant Jesus said:] 'So peace is upon me the day I was born, the day that I die, and the day that I shall be raised up to life' (19:33).

Jesus foretold the coming of Ahmad (a name of the Prophet Muhammad):

'And remember, Jesus, the son of Mary, said: "O Children of Israel! I am the messenger of Allah to you, confirming the Law [Torah] before me, and giving good news of a messenger to come after me, whose name shall be Ahmad"'(61:6).

Jesus also denies that he has called himself God.

'And behold! Allah will say: "O Jesus the son of Mary! Did you say to men: 'Worship me and my mother as gods in derogation of Allah'?" He will say: "Glory be to you! Never could I say what I had no right to say. Had I said such a thing, you

11

would indeed have known it. You know what is in my heart, though I do not know what is in yours. For you know in full all that is hidden. I never said to them anything except what you commanded me to say: 'Worship Allah, my Lord and your Lord'"'(5:116-117).

The Qur'an calls Jesus 'a Word from God' as well as 'Word of God'. Jesus is also 'a Spirit from God', but unambiguously not God's Son.

'Behold! The angels said: "O Mary! Allah gives you good news of a Word from him: his name will be Christ Jesus, the son of Mary, held in honour in this world and the hereafter, and of those nearest to Allah"'(3:45).

'O People of the Book! Commit no excesses in your religion, nor say about Allah anything but the truth. Christ Jesus, the son of Mary, was (no more than) a messenger of Allah and his Word, which he bestowed on Mary, and a Spirit proceeding from him: so believe in Allah and his messengers. Do not say 'Three': desist; it will be better for you, for Allah is one God – glory be to him, (far exalted is he) above having a son. To him belong all things in the heavens and on earth. And Allah suffices as a disposer of affairs' (4:171).

'Say: "He is Allah, the One and Only; Allah, the Eternal, Absolute; he begets not, nor is he begotten; and there is none like him"' (112).

'They are unbelievers who say: "Allah is Christ, the son of Mary." For Christ said: "O Children of Israel! Worship Allah, my Lord and your Lord"' (5:72).

'The Jews call Uzayr a son of God, and the Christians call Christ the Son of God. That is what they say with their own mouths. (In this) they only imitate what the unbelievers of old used to say. Allah's curse be on them: how they are deluded away from the truth! They take their scribes and their monks to be their lords in derogation of Allah, and (they take as their Lord) Christ, the son of Mary; yet they were commanded to worship but one God: there is no God but he. Praise and glory to him:

(far is he) from having the partners they associate (with him)' (9:30-31.)

After this survey of some of the key Qur'anic references to Jesus, it should be noted that although the Qur'an accords a position of great dignity to Jesus it in fact devotes significantly more space to both Abraham and Moses.

The Islamic theological tradition aims to set Jesus and all that is distinctive about him (his conception without a human father, his miracles, his titles 'Word of God' and 'Spirit of God') in the context of what is 'normal' for prophets. 'Before Allah, Jesus is like Adam: [Allah] created him from dust, then said to him "Be", and he was' (Qur'an 3:59). The creation of Adam with neither a father nor a mother is seen as even more miraculous than the conception of Jesus without a father. The title 'Word of God' only indicates a prophet, or alternatively the creative act of the word of God which caused Jesus to be conceived in Mary's womb. Anyway, Muhammad is a greater prophet than Jesus since Muhammad is the 'Seal of the Prophets' (Qur'an 33:40).

This description of Muhammad is paralleled by a tendency in Islamic mysticism to call Jesus the 'seal of the saints', since, while Muhammad remains 'the Seal of the Prophets', the word and the spirit of God were fully bestowed on Jesus.

More recent Muslim publications about Jesus present him as a righteous man who suffered persecution (Kâmil Hussayn); as the prophet of love (Abbâs Mahmûd Aqqâd); as the liberator of humanity (Khâlid Muhammad Khâlid); or as one who inspires a higher personality (Fathî Uthmân).

In the religious life of Muslims Jesus does not generally play an outstanding role; indeed in this respect he is less significant than Mary. To Muslim eyes, the person and role of Jesus have been exaggerated by Christians; the Christian deification of Jesus is a blasphemy. Furthermore, in the course of history Christians have repeatedly, and in the name of the cross of Christ, acted with aggression towards the Islamic world.

13

III. Christian Perspectives

1. From the earthly ministry of Jesus to the Easter faith

Recent studies of the New Testament stress that Jesus was a fully human person, but one in whom the rule of God comes near. In the preaching and in the acts of Jesus God is revealed as both his Father and our Father. Jesus was born and grew up like every other human being. After he had left his home and family in Nazareth, he was baptized by John the Baptist. This was a pivotal moment when, through the Holy Spirit, Jesus experienced God's affirmation of him as his 'beloved Son' and, simultaneously, God's commissioning of him as his 'servant'. The language used at the baptism of Jesus (e.g., at Mark 1:11) echoes Old Testament passages which speak on the one hand of the King of Israel as God's Son (e.g., Psalm 2:7) and on the other hand of a mysterious 'servant' of God through whose extreme sufferings God's salvation will be extended beyond Israel to the ends of the earth (Isaiah 42:1-7; cf. also Isaiah 49:1-7; 50:4-11; 52:13–53:12).

Jesus claimed to be more than all the prophets and the teachers of the Law who came before him. A teacher of the Law says: '*Moses* has said...' A prophet says: 'Thus says the *Lord...*' But Jesus, without appealing to any higher authority, simply says: 'Truly I tell you...' Especially striking in this regard is the sermon delivered by Jesus in his home town Nazareth (Luke 4:14-30), in which he in effect says: 'I am the one in whom what was promised through the prophets becomes reality.' Finally, in speaking of God, Jesus did not place his hearers and himself in the same position before the one whom he called 'Father'. Rather, he distinguished between 'your Father' and 'my Father'. Human beings are children of this Father, but Jesus alone is 'the Son' in an absolute sense.

Those who heard the preaching of Jesus quickly grasped that they must either accept his unprecedented claims, and therefore dedicate themselves wholly to him and his teaching, or alternatively must regard him as a blasphemer and deceiver on an extraordinary scale. Those who chose not to believe in

14

Jesus therefore behaved quite consistently by arresting him and having him executed, condemned under their own law as a blasphemer and under the law of the occupying Romans as a disturber of the peace. And they appeared to be right. Nothing happened as they mocked him on the cross: 'He saved others; he cannot save himself' (Mark 15:31).

We know what happened next. The utter despair of the disciples, who had given up all hope (Luke 24:21), did not last long. Jesus appeared to them as the Living One, risen from the dead. This caused them – and those who came to faith through their testimony – to reflect on how they could most adequately express what needed to be said about Jesus. They called him 'the Son of God'; so also they prayed to him and publicly confessed him. It is certainly possible to express what is meant thereby differently, especially today. But this title 'Son of God' was particularly appropriate for the confession and the proclamation of the faith – and it has always remained so.

Furthermore, Jesus himself hinted that this title conveys the truth. In the Gospels there are frequent passages in which either Jesus calls himself 'the Son' or others wonder whether he is 'the Son of God' (e.g., Matthew 16:16; Mark 14:61-2; Luke 1:32). And since he so emphatically calls God 'my' Father, how can it be wrong to call him 'the Son of God'?

To call Jesus 'the Son of God' was to make quite clear the claim that he is unique, more than just a man. It was enormously challenging to apply this title to Jesus because in doing so the Christian faith was eradicating all the images (whether glorious or bizarre) which the Jews and the Greeks had formed of the 'sons of the Gods'. 'The Son of God', Christians insisted, 'is none other than this Jesus – this controversial, mocked, persecuted, executed Jesus.' It is no wonder that the powerful did not tolerate this.

To call Jesus 'Lord' raised similar issues. The Greek version of the Old Testament already in use by the time of Jesus used this same word ('*Kurios*') to translate the Hebrew divine name 'Yahweh', though '*Kurios*' could also signify 'Master'. For the

Greeks 'Kurios' was a divine title, so it was natural for Caesar to adopt it for himself since he demanded veneration as a deity. Martyrdom was therefore the fate of those Christians who, resisting this veneration of Caesar, insisted: 'Jesus alone is Lord.'

2. The development of the Church's doctrine of the person of Jesus

The teaching of the Church is quite clear: Jesus Christ is the Son of God become human! Jesus is a truly human being, our brother. He is born to a human mother, grows up and matures, learns a trade, suffers hunger and thirst, displays joy and compassion, anxiety and anger. He is a human being with body and soul – truly one of us, close to us. It is this belief in the reality of the Incarnation that justifies for Christians the artistic depictions of Mary and of Jesus which are so questionable to Muslims.

Over the centuries the Church has resolutely held to this teaching. To many it appeared easier to believe in a God who only seemed to be present on this earth, only seemed to have lived and suffered. In that case, however, God would not truly have entered into our humanity, and we would only seem to have been redeemed. But God did indeed become human for the sake of all human beings, and our whole humanity is thus healed by him. Nevertheless, the Church has always at the same time confessed Jesus as 'Lord', which indicates nothing less than the divine name 'Yahweh'.

It remains central for Christian faith that the Son of God is one of us, with all that that entails, sin excepted. Jesus is therefore both divine and human in one person. For centuries Christians have struggled with the depths of the meaning of this sentence. It has been necessary to reject many heresies which have given one-sided emphasis to either the divine or the human nature in Jesus. In truth he is both fully human and fully divine, even if this cannot ultimately be explained. Fully human, with a human soul and a human will, so that through his obedient humanity he could redeem our humanity. And yet also fully God, 'of one substance with the Father' – as the Church expressed it in 325 at the Council

16

of Nicaea. Divinity and humanity are united in the person of the Redeemer. Personal experience of God thus becomes possible. The believer encounters the human Jesus Christ – and so also encounters God himself.

In response to questions from Muslims, there should be no concealing of the fact that faith in Jesus as the incarnate Son of God is an essential part of the apostolic confession of faith. Only by the working of the Holy Spirit can we acknowledge and proclaim Jesus as Lord (1 Corinthians 12:3).

Christian faith understands itself as the answer, made possible by the Holy Spirit, to the question posed by the historical person of Jesus. Since this Christian confession is an answer arising from faith, it cannot be demanded of others who do not share this faith. We must recognize that there are other interpretations of Jesus: a Marxist interpretation, for example, or that of the Brahmo Samâj (a 19th century Hindu reform movement); interpretations given by Muslims or by Jews, and so on.

In this regard two observations should be made. Firstly, respect should be shown for the claims of historical and literary criticism, at least when these are based on serious academic work and are not the product of pure imagination. Secondly, it should be acknowledged, even by those who do not share the Christian faith, that the Christian interpretation of Jesus is one of the range of possibilities.

IV. Christian Answers

1. The mysteries of the Incarnation and of the divinity of Jesus occupy a central place in the Christian faith. For Christians, the doctrine of the Incarnation does not signify the 'deification' of a man. Rather, in the Incarnation the eternal Word of God takes on a human nature and so becomes a human being. The expression 'Son of God' serves as a pointer to the divine origin of Jesus and to the fact that in Jesus God has made himself present to humanity in a unique way. It is not a biological statement, such as would make of God a parent

17

in the ordinary human sense. In this context it is worth noting a passage from the 4th Lateran Council (1215): 'This reality [the divine nature] neither begets nor is begotten'.[7] This corresponds to Qur'an 112:3: 'He begets not, nor is he begotten' (*lam yalid wa lam yûlad*). The context of this Qur'anic verse is, however, quite different as the Qur'an is here primarily protesting against Meccan polytheism, which attributed biological procreation to God, and is concerned with Christian teaching about Jesus only secondarily.

2. The point raised earlier in this chapter about the history of military aggression in the name of Christ will be addressed in chapter 9 below.

3. Between the Christian doctrine of the Incarnation and the statements of the Qur'an there are linkages which can appear significant to the Muslim. Many Muslims recognize that the Qur'an holds the central place in Islam which Jesus holds in the Christian faith. Muslims believe that the Word of God (*kalâm Allâh*) is eternally in God (*kalâm nafsî*), and is even identical with God's essence according to several theologians. It has been revealed in the form of a Scripture, the Qur'an as the Word of God 'become book' (*kalâm lafzî*). A Christian believes that Jesus is the Word of God, but in a sense different from how a Muslim understands his Qur'anic title *kalimat Allâh*. The Christian faith bears witness that Jesus of Nazareth, the crucified and risen Lord, is the final and perfect revelation of God in history.

18

Chapter 3

Cross, Sin, Redemption

1. Muslim Questions

▶ How can the eternal God suffer and die on a cross? How can God abandon to his enemies so great a prophet as Jesus? How can the Father sacrifice his Son on the cross? This is all simply blasphemy.

▶ The death of an innocent and righteous person can neither wipe away the sins of another person nor can it redeem another person from his or her sins. For an innocent person to die in the place of a guilty person is an outrageous injustice.

▶ For God to forgive sins there is absolutely no need for the 'sacrifice' of which Christianity speaks. God is almighty and forgives all people their sins, requiring only that they repent, or even just that they remain constant in their faith as Muslims. God is kind; he is not an unmerciful judge.

▶ Why must all people bear the consequences of Adam's sin and so be considered guilty? How can a newborn child be a sinner since he or she is unable to commit any sins? Isn't each individual responsible for his or her own actions?

▶ Human nature is not radically evil. Why is Christianity so pessimistic?

19

▶ Do contemporary Christian theologians refuse to accept the view that the whole Jewish people has been rejected by God because of its involvement in the violent death of Jesus?

2. Muslim Perspectives

General

Everyone is responsible for his or her own deeds and will be rewarded or punished for them individually. The ideas that children are burdened with the sins of their fathers and that someone ought to atone for the sins of others are absurd and utterly unintelligible.

Christians overstate the gravity of human sin. Sin is to be understood chiefly as the breaking of moral and social conventions (infringing on that which is beyond the bounds or *haram*) or in the worst case the breaking of the Law given by God (*sharîa*). Sin does not constitute an assault on God himself, who is too great and exalted to be able to be harmed by the sins of those whom he has created. In his omnipotence and goodness, his sovereignty and generosity, it is easy for God to forgive. One can therefore be reckoned a good Muslim even without always obeying the Law in every respect. The only unforgivable sins are idolatry (*shirk*) and apostasy (*irtidâd*), the rejection of Islam by a Muslim.

The Christian doctrine of the Incarnation is scandalous in itself; Christian claims about the Crucifixion go even further, with the idea of a God who becomes a human being and dies as one who has been cursed. The crucifixion of Christ is explicitly denied and indignantly rejected by the Qur'an.

The cross has also had disastrous effects in history. It has served as the symbol of ventures which can scarcely be regarded as witnessing to Christian love: the crusades, which in both Western languages and Arabic are linked to the word 'cross' (*salîb, al-hurûb al-salîbiyya* – wars under the banner of the cross); and Western colonialism, in which political power and Christianity have been closely entangled together. Even today, discussions of the tensions between the Islamic world and the West make frequent use of the symbols of cross and crescent.

Despite all this, even today Christians continue to adhere to their belief in the 'saving' significance of the cross. Catechisms and devotional writings still declare: 'Christ atoned for our sins... In the face of divine righteousness, Christ made satisfaction for our sins... Through the sins of Adam and Eve we all became guilty.'

Detailed

1. Humanity and Sin

The Qur'an closely parallels the biblical account of the sin of Adam (Qur'an 2:30-38; 7:19-27; 20:117-123). God commands Adam and his wife (not named as Eve in the Qur'an) not to eat from the tree of life but they sin by rejecting God's command. However, it is important to stress that in the Qur'an Adam repents and God forgives him. Adam is thus able to become the first of the line of sinless prophets.

Adam's sin has consequences for his descendants. They are shut out of Paradise; they are subjected to Satan's temptations; their common life is filled with strife. In other verses, however, the Qur'an vehemently protests against any idea of collective responsibility. The phrase is often repeated: 'No bearer of burdens can bear the burden of another...' (6:164; 7:28; 17:15; 35:18; 39:7). The fact that 'our fathers' have sinned cannot excuse our own transgression. Everyone is challenged to be conscious of his or her individual responsibility. The Last Judgement will be on a strictly individual basis; everyone will be called to account on that day. (See 52:21; 53:38; 56:4-11; 82:19 and especially 99:7-8.)

'Then anyone who has done an atom's weight of good shall see it. And anyone who has done an atom's weight of evil shall see it' (99:7-8).

Nevertheless, the Qur'an does also acknowledge that human

21

beings incline towards evil by their very nature. When the Qur'an refers to human beings in general (*al-insân*) it nearly always asserts that they are rebellious (*'âsin*), ungrateful/unbelieving (the dual meanings of *kâfir*), violent, impatient, quarrelsome and untrustworthy (2:75; 3:72; 5:61; 6:43; 7:94-5; 14:34; 17:11,67,100; 18:54-5; 21:37; 33:72; 48:26). They shed blood and cause mischief (2:30) from the first shedding of blood, the murder of one son of Adam by another (5:27-32), up to the killing of the prophets by the Children of Israel (2:61; 3:21,112,181,183; 4:155; 5:70). The Qur'an speaks of the soul as 'certainly prone to evil' (12:53).

Furthermore, the Qur'an refers to the solidarity of all human beings in sin as well as in good deeds. The wicked bring forth godlessness, those who are lost seek to direct others into error (2:109; 3:69,98,110; 5:49) and they act together against God (5:78; 8:73; 21:54). In contrast, believers show solidarity by encouraging each other to do good (4:114; 9:71; 60:10).

As regards intercession (*shafâ'a*), Muslim theologians hold that the Qur'an teaches that every prophet will offer intercession for his own people (24:62; cf. 3:159; 4:54; 8:33). Muhammad in particular will intercede for his followers, the Muslims, in response to the prayers of believers, and of course only ever 'with God's permission' (2:255; 10:3; 19:67). Among Sufis there is a notable tendency to multiply intercessors (*walî*, pl. *awliyâ'* – saints, friends of God), but at the risk of encouraging superstition and incurring the disapproval of the theologians.

2. The Cross

The Qur'an explicitly denies the death of Jesus on the cross

'They [the Jews] did not kill him, neither did they crucify him: but so it was made to appear to them [*'shubbiha lahum'*]' (4:157; cf. 3:55).

The usual interpretation by the Qur'anic commentators of the phrase '*shubbiha lahum*' takes it as meaning that somebody was substituted for Jesus and was crucified in his place. Among the various substitutes suggested by the Hadith and the Qur'anic commentators we find the leader of the Romans, Simon of Cyrene, Peter and Judas Iscariot. In the Muslim tradition taken as a whole there is no doubt that Jesus was not crucified; rather God, protecting Jesus from his enemies, took him away beyond their reach and raised Jesus up to himself in heaven. Jesus will come again at the end of time to proclaim the imminent arrival of the Last Day.

It is important to understand why the Qur'an and Islam deny an event which is otherwise reckoned as a certain historical fact. More than the influence of Docetic or Gnostic tendencies, it is the distinctive monotheism of the Qur'an itself which leads to the conclusion that Jesus did not die on the cross. Many of the stories in the Qur'an which deal with the line of prophets are cast in one and the same form: the prophet is sent to his nation but is rejected by all except a small number; the people seek to kill him but he is miraculously saved by God, because God cannot surrender his own envoy to his enemies. It should be acknowledged that in the Medinan period the Qur'an does criticize the Children of Israel, the forefathers of the Jews of Medina, for having killed the prophets sent to them, but these are a few brief references while the dominant pattern in the Qur'an is of prophets delivered by God from the hands of their enemies, vindicated over against unbelievers. The story of Jesus follows exactly this pattern.

3. The Forgiveness of Sins

The Qur'an often presents God as abundantly forgiving. The sinner's repentance and God's forgiveness are closely linked; indeed, God's forgiveness even goes before human repentance and is its cause (9:118). Muslim theologians teach that repentance wipes sins away: this happens almost 'automatically' according to the Mutazilites, but only 'if God wills' in the view of the Asharites, who paradoxically go on to say that human repentance and divine forgiveness are strictly unrelated. If a person repents, his or her sins are wiped away; but even if he or she does not repent, God can still forgive. In any case, the Asharite doctrine holds that whoever maintains in his or her heart 'an atom of [Muslim] faith' will enter Paradise. In contrast, the Qur'an and modern Islamic theologians insist on the importance of good deeds.

III. Christian Perspectives

1. 'Original Sin'

Most contemporary Christian biblical scholars and theologians agree on the meaning of Genesis 3 and Romans 5:12-21. These texts do not present a scholarly account of the origins of the human race and of the stages of human evolution, but rather, through symbolic narrative, they express convictions which arise through general observation of evil and sin in the world.

As long as human beings have been on the earth – however one might explain their origins – sin has been present: individual and corporate selfishness; murderous conflicts; rebellion against God and his commandments; idolatry. All people experience in themselves the struggle between the good which they would like to do and the evil which attracts them (Romans 7:21-25). This attractive power of evil is at work right at the heart of our humanity. From birth onwards, it is present in every child. The instinctive experience of the human race is not only of being in harmony and friendship with God but also of 'inheriting' a 'nature' moulded by a long history of good and evil and especially by a network of personal guilt. This all undermines the possibility of understanding and unity both among human beings and between them and God. This whole situation is summarized in the biblical expression 'the sin of the world' (John 1:29). So Paul comes to the conclusion: every person, whether Jew or Gentile, is dependent on the forgiving grace of God which has been revealed in Jesus Christ (cf. Romans 3:21-25; Ephesians 2:8-9). In baptism, believers place themselves under the lordship of Christ, and in him the power of sin is broken; the thinking here is of sin as a milieu, environment or dominating power, not as individual, personal acts.

24

The language of 'original sin' therefore does not refer to a personal sin which would make every human being guilty from birth onwards. Neither in the Bible nor in the official teaching of the Church is there anything that allows us to speak of the transmission of personal guilt. The prophet Ezekiel (chapter 18) protests vehemently against this idea, which is also rejected by Jesus (Matthew 16:27; John 9:2-3).

2. Cross and Redemption

Belief in redemption through the cross has in reality led to some questionable ways of thinking and some unhealthy forms of religious practice: whether a kind of spiritual glorification of suffering ('*dolorismus*') which at times leads to masochism; or the ideal of a passive obedience; or a mentality which seeks to make calculations about divine justice; or the demand for reparation through voluntary suffering of punishment in place of others, and so on. One could even add to this category the way in which some contemporary revolutionary leaders praise the ultimate sacrifice of a person's life in the 'holy' struggle for justice and liberation. It is therefore appropriate to call to mind some basic Christian truths.

2.1 The cross as the consequence of Jesus' life

The life of Jesus is itself liberating and redemptive. He displayed inner freedom towards the practice in his day of the religious Law, which had in part been interpreted contrary to the original will of God and so laid unnecessary burdens on people (cf. Matthew 11:28; 23:4; Luke 11:46). This approach, along with the faithfulness with which Jesus revealed the true face of God as a father who loves all people without preconditions, brought upon him the hostility of the leaders of his people. Collaborating with those who had become disillusioned with Jesus, these leaders condemned him to death. They handed him over to the power of the Romans who killed him in accordance with their laws, employing the traditional, cruel punishment of crucifixion. The violent death of Jesus was the inevitable consequence of all that he had set in motion in his life.

The death of Jesus on the cross seemed to his opponents to pass definitive judgement on him: his claims could not have had any genuine base in reality, because otherwise he ought not to have been abandoned to die by God and the whole world. The disciples, who had believed that in Jesus God himself had been present and active and God's kingdom had come near, appeared to have been deceived. What Jesus had taught about God must have been wrong.

If the disciples do not remain in this state of disillusionment but again confess Jesus to be the one who reveals God, this must rest on the fact that their eyes have been opened and they see Jesus, the Crucified One, in a new way and are therefore able to encounter him in a new way.

The death of Jesus on the cross must therefore not be regarded as indicating that he was wrong to proclaim God as unconditional love and to behave accordingly. As Erhard Kunz, S.J. has written:

The death of Jesus can also be understood precisely as an intrinsic and profound consequence of this very love, so that Jesus' fundamental vision is not disproved by the cross but rather is validated by it. For whoever loves and is good to another person, without demanding preconditions as to how that love and goodness should be demonstrated, will stay by the other person's side, regardless of changing circumstances, showing devotion to the other even when – particularly when – the other is in danger. Whoever loves in the way of Jesus does not shun suffering and hold back from it but rather shares in it, showing compassion, the literal meaning of which is to 'suffer with'. In a dangerous and needy world love leads us into suffering (cf. Luke 10:30-37). So love as Jesus understood it does not separate itself off from those who have fallen into evil. It bears the evil and seeks to overcome it through good. By enduring injustice and violence without becoming embittered, such love breaks the vicious circle based on the principle of retaliation ('An eye for an eye'!). Faced by the kind of love that does not strike back when it is struck, evil comes to a standstill. Love thus conquers evil. In an evil world love therefore leads to the suffering of unjust violence, and in the most extreme case to the suffering of an unjust death (cf. Matthew 5:38-48).

If Jesus wishes to bear convincing witness to God as unconditional and boundless love in a suffering and evil world, then he cannot avoid enduring unjust violence. So the encounter with danger and violence does not undermine Jesus' fundamental vision but on the contrary is the way in which, in our world, unconditional love must generally take effect. The good towards which love aspires can only be attained in our world through compassion and through the suffering which overcomes evil. Only when the grain of wheat falls into the earth and dies can it bear fruit (John 12:24). From this perspective the death of Jesus on the cross appears not as a fatal end, revealing all that had gone before to be mere illusion, but as the necessary fulfilment of the ministry of Jesus. In his suffering and death Jesus loves to the utmost extent (John 13:1).[8]

2.2 The redemptive significance of the death of Jesus in the light of the Resurrection

By raising Jesus from the dead, God confirms the inner meaning which he had given to Jesus' life and death. By raising him from death to life God makes Jesus present to the lives of all people of all times. The significance of the life and death of Jesus is therefore made present to us and effective among us as 'something contemporary'. Because Jesus as the Risen One is alive and present in God, he is able today, just as in his life before the Resurrection, to communicate to people God's forgiving love. As the Risen One he has the power to liberate from sin and death. Consequently every person is redeemed insofar as he or she chooses, wittingly or unwittingly, to enter into the life of Jesus: i.e. with and in Jesus to live out the same faithfulness to the truth that comes from God; to love the brothers and sisters to the point of laying down one's life; and to extend unconditional forgiveness to opponents and enemies. Thus the chain of hatred, whose power binds both wrongdoers and their victims, is broken. In brief: through the Resurrection of Jesus God makes love triumph over hatred.

Jesus is Lord, Saviour and Redeemer through his Resurrection, which transforms his exemplary life and his death into a power which can liberate from the chains of sin and death, and makes it possible for people to enter into the life of the Son of God.

We can therefore say with Scripture: Jesus dies not only 'for the sake of our sins', i.e., as the victim of and sacrifice for the misunderstandings, the selfishness and the hatred that are so universally present and are always with us, but also 'for us sinners', i.e., to open up for us the way to liberation from our sins and to give us the strength and grace to attain this liberation.

2.3 Early Christian reflection on the life and death of Jesus

The disciples of Jesus, both women and men, were utterly astonished by the Resurrection. After they had been convinced of the decisive failure and destruction of this prophet, they were overpowered by the experience of the presence of the risen Jesus in the Holy Spirit. They now proclaim that he is 'Lord and Redeemer'. It is quite natural that they seek an explanation of his scandalous death and that they should be helped in this by the patterns of biblical thought available to them: for example, the theme of the great witness or martyr, who in his free and total self-dedication attests to his faithfulness to the mission given to him by the Father (John 10:18; 18:37; cf. Revelation 1:5; 3:14); the theme of the suffering servant who dies for the sins of his people (Isaiah 50:5-8; 53:1-12); the theme of the Redeemer, Yahweh himself, the *gö'ël*, who redeems his people by liberating them from slavery in Egypt and 'purchasing' or 'ransoming' them as his people (Exodus 6:6-8; cf. 2 Samuel 7:23f.; Jeremiah 31:32); and finally the theme of the perfect sacrifice, in which the victim offers himself and so takes the place of the animal sacrifices previously offered (Hebrews 7:27; 9:12,26,28; 10:10; 12-14; cf. Romans 6:10; 1 Peter 3:18).

This effort by the early Christians to make the death of Jesus intelligible in the light of his Resurrection permeated the different writings of the New Testament. The vocabulary of the Christian tradition developed out of this process of reflection, from Hebrew to Greek, Latin and other languages and their respective cultures: martyrdom, deliverance, redemption, atonement, sacrifice, reparation, substitution.

2.4 Theologies of redemption

Building on this vocabulary, and also partially detaching it from its biblical roots, theologies of redemption have made use of the cultural contexts of their times, with particular attention paid to the judicial categories so dear to the Latin West. This process has given rise to the following theories, among others:

1. The punishment theory (the Latin Fathers, Augustine [354-430]). Sin demands a punishment equivalent to the offence. Christ takes the punishment upon himself and redeems us by settling the debt owing to the divine justice. Some Fathers go so far as to say that Christ paid the debt to the devil, who had taken possession of the human race.

2. The theological theories of substitution or satisfaction (Tertullian c. 160–c. 220; Anselm of Canterbury (1033 – 1109). Sin is transgression against God. Since God is infinite, transgression against him demands infinite reparation, which finite human beings are not in a position to offer. In his love God therefore provides an intermediary by substituting his own Son for human beings. The Son can thus satisfy the divine justice.

3. Leading mediaeval theologians, particularly Thomas Aquinas (1225-1274), expounded the loving purposes contained within the work of redemption. God could have forgiven our sins directly, but to forgive so simply would have indicated that he ascribed little worth to the human race created by him 'in his image' and as his steward (*khalīfa*) on earth. God wanted human beings to partake in his saving and forgiving action, first of all in Christ, who is truly human, and secondly

– through and in Christ – in every human being. By being 'supernaturally' raised up into the life of Christ through pure grace, every human being is able to co-operate in the perfecting of his or her redemption, living and dying in willing submission to God after the pattern of the willing submission of Christ. Such a Christ-like life will be marked by faith, repentance and obedience to the voice of conscience.

From these and other theologies we ought to hold on to the effort to convey: the 'weighty' character of the process of redemption (Punishment theory); the fact that Christ took upon himself a sinful humanity and accepted its consequences (Substitution); the participation of human beings in their own redemption (Merit); Christ's voluntary laying down of his life (Sacrifice). We can, however, dispense with the judicial frames of reference of these theories. But above all we should not separate the death of Jesus on the cross from his life and Resurrection.

IV. Christian Answers

Original sin is not personal sin or guilt inherited from Adam. Original sin refers to the general environment which prevails because of the sins in the world, an environment to which every human being is subject from birth onwards. Sin itself is a personal act for which everybody is individually responsible. We can ignore neither the inclination to evil within ourselves, nor the bad influences which can tempt us in the direction of evil. There are also social outworkings of sin, increasing the power of evil in the world.

The death of Jesus on the cross is a historical fact which there are no good reasons for denying. I believe, however, that I can understand the reasons which cause the Qur'an to deny it. The Qur'an denies the death of Jesus on the cross in order to make clear God's gracious providence for those who are his own. It is therefore important to explain that according to the Christian faith God did not abandon Jesus on the cross but raised him from the dead and transformed his death into glory.

Furthermore, it is not the case that God 'delivers Jesus to death' as if performing a dramatic script written beforehand, in which all participants simply play their roles like puppets. Jesus was condemned to death by human beings because of the attitude displayed in his life towards God and the Law. He was the victim of evil powers: hatred, injustice, envy, self-interest – powers which still mould this world.

The 2nd Vatican Council (1962-1965) stated emphatically that the sins of all people were ultimately responsible for the death of Jesus. The Council refused to assign responsibility for the rejection and killing of Jesus to the descendants of the Jews of the time of Jesus or indeed to all Jewish people, past and present.[9]

Redemption is not the appeasement of a vengeful God who, in order to restore his lost honour, demands the sacrifice of an innocent person to bring about atonement on behalf of those who are guilty. Redemption is about the powerful revelation of the forgiving and compassionate love of God in the life, death and Resurrection of Jesus, who, by laying down his life for those whom he loves, gives to human beings the gift of fellowship with God and enables them to live lives empowered by love.

Chapter 4

Muhammad and the Christian Faith

I. Muslim Questions

Islam recognizes all prophets. It certainly distinguishes between them, seeing some as more important than others, but it sees them all as bearers of the truth of the one same message. Jesus is one of the prophets (2:136,285; 3:84).

▶ In the same way as Muslims, do you Christians recognize all prophets as such, including Muhammad?

II. Muslim Perspectives

General

The Qur'an mentions many prophets who were sent by God in the course of history, one after another. Jesus is one of the greatest among them (2:136,253, etc). However, the sequence of prophets reaches its conclusion and fulfilment in Muhammad, the 'Seal of the Prophets' (33:40). The Islamic faith consequently recognizes in the revelation of the Qur'an the criterion of truth in all religious questions.

Muslims feel offended when Christians deny to Muhammad the status of a prophet. Furthermore, Muslims feel that by denying the prophethood of Muhammad, whom God himself chose to be the bearer of the Qur'an for the whole human race, Christians also deny the religious, spiritual and mystical value of Islam, i.e., the living religious practice both of Muslims in general and also of their specific Muslim partners in dialogue. Muslims also experience this rejection as an insult to the person whom they have been taught to respect and love from their earliest childhood. This feeling is often strengthened when the Muslim dialogue partner is familiar with the negative judgements on Muhammad which have a long tradition in Christian literature and theology, where Muhammad is sometimes portrayed as a liar and a deceiver.

Detailed

From the beginning, the Qur'an claims to be delivering the same monotheistic message which God had already bestowed upon earlier prophets and which now in the Qur'an is communicated 'in clear Arabic language'. The Qur'an mentions 25 such prophets by name, the names of most of them being familiar to us from the biblical tradition. After Adam come Enoch (*Idrîs*), Noah (*Nûh*), Abraham (*Ibrahîm*), Isaac (*Ishâq*), Ishmael (*Isma'îl*), Lot (*Lût*), Jacob (*Ya'qûb*), Joseph (*Yûsuf*), Jethro (*Shu'ayb*), Moses (*Mûsâ*), Aaron (*Hârûn*), David (*Dâwûd*), Solomon (*Sulaimân*), Elijah (*Ilyâs*), Elisha (Al-*yâsâ*), Isaiah (*Dhûlkifl*), Jonah (*Yûnus*), Job (*Ayyûb*), Zechariah (*Zakariyya*) and his son John (*Yahyâ*) the Baptist, and Jesus (*Îsâ*), the son of Mary. Mary is not called a prophet in the Qur'an and is not generally reckoned as such by Muslims but she is accorded great respect and is indeed the only woman to be named in the Qur'an. Apart from Elijah, Elisha, Isaiah, Jonah and Moses (on some occasions), these characters are not normally reckoned as prophets in the Bible. On the other hand, the four 'major' and the twelve 'minor' biblical prophets – apart from Isaiah and Jonah – are not mentioned in the Qur'an, and Jonah is only mentioned in the context of the story of the great fish that swallowed him. There are also Qur'anic prophets unknown in the Bible, notably Hûd the prophet of the tribe of 'Âd, and Sâlih, the prophet of the tribe of Thamûd.

Three of the Qur'anic prophets are dealt with in particular detail. They are the central characters in numerous Qur'anic narratives, which sometimes call to mind biblical passages but also sometimes differ from these considerably.

Abraham is ready, in obedience to God, to sacrifice his son, who is not named in the Qur'an but who all Muslims now believe was Ishmael rather than Isaac, as in the Bible. He greets and welcomes the angels sent to him by God. He is a striking and perfect model of monotheistic faith. He purifies Meccan worship from polytheism and together with his son Ishmael lays the foundation stone of the Kaaba.[10] Uniquely among the prophets it is thus Abraham who shapes the prayers and the spirit of the Hajj (the pilgrimage prescribed for Muslims in the Qur'an).

Moses is saved from the waters of the Nile and brought up at the court of Pharaoh. Later, with the help of his brother Aaron, he obtains permission for his people to leave Egypt. After the crossing of the Red Sea on dry ground, on Mount Sinai God speaks to Moses (who is thus known as *kalîm Allâh*) and God entrusts to him the Torah (i.e., the five books of Moses).

Jesus is born to the Virgin Mary in a miraculous way (under a palm tree in the desert); he receives from God the Gospel (*Injîl* – a single book); preaches monotheism to the Sons of Israel; performs various miracles (for example, giving life to a bird made out of clay, revealing secret thoughts, healing the blind and lepers, raising the dead to life). He is confronted with the hostility of the Jews, who even claim to have crucified him. That, however, is an illusion, because God raised Jesus to himself in heaven before the Jews could carry out their plan. Jesus is alive and will come again at the end of time as a forerunner preparing the way for the Day of Judgement, and proclaiming that Islam is the true religion. During his life he foretells the coming of the last of the prophets, who will bear the name Ahmad (61:6; this name is equivalent to Muhammad). He is 'Word of God' and 'Spirit of God', but neither Son of God nor God himself.

The greatest of all the prophets is Muhammad himself, the 'Seal of the Prophets'. He was born in Mecca 570 years after Christ. When he was forty years old, this successful merchant received revelations urging him to go forth as a prophet and to proclaim afresh the will of the one God. His words – understood as direct revelation from the 'preserved tablet' in heaven – were

35

gathered together in the Qur'an. In 622 Muhammad escaped from the persecution of the Meccans through the Hijra[11] to Yathrib (later called Medina). There he became not only a religious but also a political leader, uniting all Muslims in their faith in the one God and bringing them together into one community (*Umma*), which transcended all tribal divisions and, despite some setbacks, steadily grew in power. Muhammad hoped to win Jews and Christians over to his message, which he saw as fulfilling rather than supplanting their own faith, but this hope was not realized. Matters came to a breaking point and Muhammad changed the direction for prayer from Jerusalem to the Kaaba in Mecca. In 630 Muhammad destroyed the idols, paintings and religious symbols in Mecca, which in 632 was the destination for the great pilgrimage, led by Muhammad himself; this established the tradition of pilgrimages which have taken place annually ever since. Muhammad died in 632. Alongside the Qur'an, Muhammad's life and pattern of behaviour provide a model for Muslims. After the death of his wife Khadîja, he was married to a number of wives at the same time. According to Islamic Tradition, he was illiterate, which serves to emphasize that Muhammad owed his teaching entirely to revelation, without any contribution from himself.

It is noteworthy that many of the stories of the prophets in the Qur'an follow the same outline:

◆ a prophet is chosen by God from among that prophet's own people;

◆ the prophet speaks his people's language;

◆ he proclaims that there is only one God (the same message that all the prophets teach);

◆ from his people he experiences hostility and is even threatened with death;

◆ God saves the one whom he has sent and punishes the unbelieving people.

This outline fully corresponds with the experience of Muhammad, which appears to be related to the Qur'anic accounts of his forerunners among the prophets. Thus the Qur'anic Jesus, like Muhammad, is a preacher of monotheism and, quite consistently, rejects the idea, put in his mouth by others, that he and his mother are gods beside Allah (5:116-117).

In Medina, after the Hijra, Muhammad encountered hostility from the local Jewish tribes and also, to a much smaller extent, from Christians. His message is related to the biblical tradition, but with a rather different emphasis. Muhammad therefore saw himself and his community as the only true followers of Abraham and rejected the claims of Jews and Christians to stand in the tradition of Abraham, who was 'neither a Jew nor a Christian', but rather the model champion of monotheism, which Muhammad was now renewing and restoring (2:135,140). Further, Muhammad saw himself as the heir of a genuine prophetic tradition, which in himself, as 'Seal of the Prophets' (33:40), found its high point and its fulfilment. The message entrusted to him, the Qur'an, was thus the criterion for measuring all previous Holy Scriptures: Torah (*Tawrât*), Psalms (*Zabûr*), Gospel (*Injîl*). According to Qur'anic teaching these Scriptures were incorrectly understood, changed, even corrupted (*tahrîf*) and no longer exist in their original purity. In consequence, Islam is now the one true, uncorrupted religion.

III. Christian Perspectives

The divine gift of prophecy is an essential element of the biblical tradition in both Old and New Testaments.[12] It reaches its highest point in Christ, who is the Word of God in human form and the prophet *par excellence*. Jesus Christ is 'the pioneer and perfecter of our faith' (Hebrews 12:2). Prophecy has its continuation in the Church, which remains prophetic to the end of time, not only through the teaching which it carries out but also in the totality of its life as the people of God, inspired by the Holy Spirit.

However, the spirit of prophecy can be active beyond the bounds of the visible Church, as was already the case with holy men and women in the Old Testament such as Melchizedek, Job and the Queen of Sheba. Justin, the 2nd-century martyr, discerned in a number of philosophers and Gentile soothsayers (such as the Sibylls) the presence of 'seeds of the Word'.[13]

More recently some theologians have gone even further. For example, during the 2nd Muslim-Christian meeting in Tunis (1979), Claude Geffré (Professor at the Catholic Institute in Paris) publicly expressed his opinion that the revelation that came through Muhammad was *a word of God*, while Christ, who is more than a prophet, is in himself *the Word of God*. Subsequently, the theologians belonging to GRIC (Groupe de Recherche Islamo-Chrétien, founded in 1977) acknowledged the presence in the Qur'an of 'a word of God, genuine but different...' from the Word of God in Jesus Christ. The differences and indeed the contradictions (for example, the Qur'anic denial of mysteries so central to the Christian faith as the Incarnation and the Trinity) were to be seen as the result of human mediation, the channel through which God's word must inevitably pass.[14]

Among theologians in other Christian traditions we encounter similar developments. In Kenneth Cragg's study *Muhammad and the Christian* (1987), this Anglican bishop and renowned scholar of Islam invites Christians to acknowledge openly that Muhammad was truly a prophet, while at the same time maintaining that Jesus is 'more than a prophet'.[15]

The 2nd Vatican Council did not make a definitive statement on this matter but it did encourage a transition to a general spirit of openness towards Islam on the part of the Church, without, however, ever mentioning Muhammad by name. It declared that 'the Church regards Muslims with esteem' (this was indeed something new!) and mentions the Islamic doctrines and rites which deserve such esteem, without denying the essential differences. By challenging Christians to esteem Muslims as believers and monotheistic worshippers, the Council implicitly rejects all the polemical and negative assertions of the past about Muhammad.[16] For he is the founder of this community and its 'beautiful pattern (of conduct)', as the Qur'an says (33:21). Whenever meetings with Muslims have occurred, Popes Paul VI (1897-1978) and John Paul II (1920-2005) have furthered this spirit of brotherliness within faith in the one God, most strikingly in John Paul II's addresses to the Christians of Turkey (Ankara, November 1979) and to young Muslims in Casablanca's stadium (17 August 1985), where the Pope spoke of genuine spiritual brotherhood between Christianity and Islam.

Regional bishops' conferences and theological seminars have made similar statements. For example, the 1971 International Theological Conference at Nagpur in India made the general claim that 'the scriptures and rites of the religions of the world can, to varying degrees, be bearers of divine revelation and paths to salvation'. In his address at the opening session of the 2nd Christian-Muslim Congress of Cordoba (March 1977), Cardinal Tarancon, at that time Archbishop of Madrid and Chairman of the Conference of Spanish Bishops, invited Christians to acknowledge the prophetic status of Muhammad, particularly because of his faith in God, his struggle against polytheism and his thirst for righteousness. As early as the 8th century the Nestorian Patriarch Timothy spoke in similar terms in the course of his dialogue in Baghdad with the Caliph al-Mahdi, saying: 'Muhammad walked in the way of the prophets'.

Christians have thus been encouraged to acknowledge the religious and ethical values which have been apparent in Muslims from the beginning and remain so today, but without at the same time removing anything essential from their own Christian faith. The way can therefore be open for Christians to recognize in the Qur'an a word from God and in the mission of Muhammad something prophetic.

IV. Christian Answers

1. We are convinced that a true dialogue can only take place on the level of true partnership, and that respect for the faith of the other is an essential component of such dialogue. Thus, just as a Christian cannot demand as a prerequisite for true dialogue that a Muslim must first believe that Jesus is the Son of God, so also a Muslim cannot demand of a Christian that he should first believe that Muhammad is 'the

Seal of the Prophets' and that the Qur'an is the final and definitive criterion for all Scriptures. For this would mean that a Christian would have to become a Muslim before inter-religious dialogue could begin (or vice versa), and indeed that inter-religious dialogue in general could not take place.[17]

2. Christians honour most of the prophets named in the Qur'an. However, the Bible also knows a wide range of other prophets, among whom some, such as Isaiah, Jeremiah and Ezekiel, are of particular significance. On the other hand, some of the prophets mentioned in the Qur'an belong exclusively to the Arab tradition and are not mentioned in the Bible. However, beyond questions about how many prophets there were, what they were called, and what exactly they proclaimed, Christians and Muslims are united by a shared belief in the one God 'who has spoken to the human race', as the 2nd Vatican Council puts it.[18] Christians and Muslims therefore base their faith not only on a philosophical approach to the discovery of God, but much more on the word which comes to them from God through the prophets; they receive this word in faith – God from God, so to say – and submit themselves to it ('submission' being the precise meaning of *islâm*, while *muslim* means 'one who submits').

3. The essential difference between Christianity and Islam is as follows. For the Muslim, prophetic revelation reaches its highest point and its conclusion in Muhammad, 'the Seal of the Prophets'; for the Christian, revelation reaches its highest point in Jesus Christ, the Word of God become human, dying on the cross and as risen Lord representing revelation in its fullness (*pleroma*). One should therefore avoid calling Jesus 'the Seal of the Prophets' as this title has specifically Islamic content and its use would hinder rather than promote inter-religious dialogue.

4. However, the fact that the Christian faith recognizes the fullness of revelation in Jesus does not prevent Christians from acknowledging that God has also made himself known to humanity elsewhere, both before and after Jesus. As

regards the Qur'an and Muhammad, it is possible to acknowledge that the Qur'an contains a word of God, and not only for Muslims but for all people, and so also for me personally. Indeed, in the Qur'an's powerful proclamation of the one transcendent God I can acknowledge that an essential element of the message of Jesus himself is recalled, and also that I am invited to live in deeper agreement with that message. Giving a believing Christian response to the message proclaimed in the Qur'an, I thus acknowledge that Muhammad was sent by God to proclaim an essential aspect of the truth, namely the oneness and transcendence of God. This is an enormously significant aspect of the truth, not least in the modern world, with its widespread forgetfulness of God.

5. As Christians and Muslims find themselves witnessing together to this foundational truth and joining in shared submission (*islâm*) to God's work – as this has been communicated to us through our respective revelations – and as Christians and Muslims grasp God's plan and will for the world more deeply and witness to them more effectively, they will themselves become bearers of this prophetic word for our world.

Excursus

Jacques Jomier, O.P., a significant Christian theologian and scholar of Islam, offers some noteworthy reflections on the meaning of Muhammad for Christianity.[19] At the time of Muhammad, Christianity required a reform, a renewal in the Spirit of Jesus. Jomier thus proposes to speak of Muhammad from a Christian perspective as a reformer, ascribing to him the charisma of a *guide réformiste*. In contrast, it would be somewhat confusing for Christians to apply to Muhammad the concept of 'prophet' (understood both from the perspective of Christian theology and also with the normative sense that it has for Islam).

1. If the concept 'prophet' is understood in an absolute sense, it indicates a person whose words, when he is speaking in the name of God, are all endowed with divine authority and

should be universally obeyed. Understood in this sense, the title 'prophet' cannot be ascribed to the founder of Islam by Christians. Christians, as such, cannot obey Muhammad unreservedly; if they did, they would be Muslims. It is not possible for Christians to accept Muhammad as a prophet in the strict sense, i.e., to believe in him and to obey him. Christians can use the title 'prophet' with reference to Muhammad only with certain limitations; in other words, they cannot accept everything that this prophet says, but rather will accept some things and reject others. For Muslims it is clearly objectionable to take such a selective approach to Muhammad, whom they regard as a true prophet, and indeed the last of the true prophets.

2. Christians accept as an aspect of the general history narrated by the Bible that the Hebrew prophets, who prepared the way for the coming of Christ, occupy a unique position. Even minor prophets, such as Zephaniah, share in this uniqueness; although they are known as 'minor' prophets, they have their place in the overall sequence of prophets which is part of the Hebrew tradition. They, along with the texts which go back to them, inspire the totality of the faith of the Church. In a religious and theological sense, the title 'prophet' should therefore not be used of Muhammad by Christians; if it is used it would be in a very limited sense which is unacceptable to Muslim faith. So it is preferable for Christians to take a different perspective on Muhammad: acknowledging the truths within the message of Islam; acknowledging and respecting the spiritual path followed by Muslims; and acknowledging that Muhammad was a religious and political genius. We should acknowledge that through God's grace at work within Islam – formed by the Qur'an and the example of Muhammad – countless believers live out a genuine relationship with God.

3. Finally, it is possible to interpret Islam, considered in the context of the history of religions, as an attempt at radical reform of Judaism and Christianity, but so radical as to involve the distorting of the essential aspects of both of these

traditions. Roughly speaking – and *mutatis mutandis* – one might compare Islam (and its prophet Muhammad) with other major reform movements in the course of history. Islam arose in an environment influenced by Judaism and Christianity, but it was a Christianity torn apart by divisions and doctrinal disputes. However, out of the reform of Judaism and Christianity brought about by Muhammad there arose a new and independent movement. This movement cast light on certain aspects of the current forms of Judaism and Christianity, for example the exclusive unity, transcendence and sovereignty of God, and the invitation to all people to receive salvation; but it rejected other, essential elements of these faiths. Could it not be that at that particular time and in that particular context Islam was entrusted with the task of prompting the Church to reform itself? If we can accept this, it need not at all mean, however, that we must deny those truths which did not find their way into Islam.[20]

Chapter 5

God, the Three in One

Muslim Questions

▸ Are you really monotheists (*muwahhidûn*)?
▸ Do you believe in three gods?
▸ Who are these gods?
▸ How can God be called Father or Son?

Muslim Perspectives

General

1. At the centre of the Islamic faith stands thoroughgoing monotheism:

   'Say: "He is Allah, the One and Only; Allah, the Eternal, Absolute; he begets not, nor is he begotten; and there is none like him"' (Qur'an 112).

2. Islam is deeply convinced about this: it is not possible to comprehend God through all too human words such as 'Father' and 'Son' which indicate primarily 'fleshly' realities. Christians have become so accustomed to giving a spiritual meaning to both these words that they have perhaps forgotten their more obvious sense.

3. The theological explanation of the Trinity through the concepts 'nature' (*tabî a*) and 'person' (*shakhs, uqnûm*) does not greatly help. Of the Arabic equivalents for person, *shakhs*

conveys the idea of a visible form, while *uqnûm* (the technical term used in Arabic Christian theological writing) is unfamiliar to contemporary Arabs. *Tabî a* refers to a created nature.

4. The Qur'an understands the Christian doctrine of God the Three in One as tritheism and refers to Christians taking Allah, Jesus and Mary as three deities – an approach which the Qur'anic Jesus himself specifically condemns:

'And behold! Allah will say: "O Jesus the son of Mary! Did you say to men: 'Worship me and my mother as gods in derogation of Allah'?" He will say: "Glory be to you! Never could I say what I had no right to say. Had I said such a thing, you would indeed have known it. You know what is in my heart, though I do not know what is in yours. For you know in full all that is hidden"' (Qur'an 5:116).

5. The Qur'an makes no reference to the Christian doctrine of the Holy Spirit as the third person of the Trinity.

Detailed

1. For the Qur'an, Christians and Jews are 'People of the Book' (*ahl al-kitâb*). On the basis of the Qur'an it remains an open question, however, whether Christians are to be considered as monotheists (2:62; 3:110-115; 4:55; 5:69,82), as unbelievers (*kuffâr.* 5:17,72-73; 9:30), or as idolaters (literally 'associators' [*mushrikûn*]: 5:72; 9:31).

2. The Qur'an reproaches Christians for saying 'three' (*thalâtha*) with reference to God (4:171). They say that God is 'the third of three' (5:73), which would seem to include Jesus and Mary (5:116)[21]. They say that Jesus is God (5:72,116), or the Son of God (9:30, using the Arabic word *ibn* for 'son'; 19:34-35, using the word *walad*), although in truth the one and only God 'begets not, nor is he begotten' (*lam yalid wa lam yûlad*, 112:3).

3. Muslim exegetes and theologians have taken a wide range of views of the Christian understanding of God. Fakhr al-dîn Râzi (1149-1209), one of the great Qur'anic commentators

of the classical period, acknowledges that no Christians of his day are of the opinion that Mary belongs to the Trinity: the Qur'anic reference must be to the version of the Christian faith of a sect no longer in existence. Many modern scholars have followed Râzi on this point.

4. One also finds among Muslim theologians some astonishingly perceptive accounts of the doctrine of the three divine persons. Many even acknowledge that Christianity is a genuine form of monotheism. The fact remains, however, that most Muslims take the view that Christians are tritheists.

Christian Perspectives

1. Who is God?

Christians are thoroughgoing monotheists and have the task of defending the monotheism which they have received from Israel. God is one. Within this frame of reference they believe that God has revealed himself as Lord and Saviour through and in Jesus Christ. This assumes that God has made himself present in Jesus Christ, but that does not mean that God has made the totality of himself present in Jesus Christ, leaving nothing as remainder. The humanity in Jesus does not absorb the divinity and the divinity does not abolish the humanity. From the beginnings of Christianity onwards these points were the basis of the theological reflection and the spiritual experience which led to the doctrine of the Trinity. The Good News (*Evangelium*) which we have received from Jesus is not only that God exists and that he is one; it also tells us *who God is*. Jesus leads his disciples into loving knowledge of God and into fellowship with him:

> Then, after speaking in many places and varied ways through the prophets, God "last of all in these days has spoken to us by his Son" (Hebrews 1:1-2). For He sent His Son, the eternal Word, who enlightens all men, so that He might dwell among men and tell them the innermost realities about God (cf. John 1:1-18). Jesus Christ, therefore, the Word made flesh, sent as "a man to men" (*Epistle to Diognetus* VII.4), "speaks the

47

words of God" (John 3:34), and completes the work of salvation which His Father gave him to do (cf. John 5:36; 17:4). To see Jesus is to see His Father (John 14:9). For this reason Jesus perfected revelation by fulfilling it through His whole work of making Himself present and manifesting Himself through His words and deeds, His signs and wonders, but especially through His death and glorious Resurrection from the dead and final sending of the Spirit of truth. Moreover, He confirmed with divine testimony what revelation proclaimed: that God is with us to free us from the darkness of sin and death, and to raise us up to life eternal.[22]

2. Father – Son

Working on the basis of the deeds, the behaviour and the words of Jesus, the first inspired witnesses (apostles and evangelists) used the word 'Son' to indicate the unique relationship between Jesus of Nazareth and the one whom he called his Father and to whom he prayed in the words 'Abba Father'. They saw in the deeds of Jesus that he claimed to exercise truly divine power, for instance in forgiving sins. They therefore concluded that there is a distinction in God between the origin of all things, the source of being and life (the Father), and the one to whom this source gives life, the firstborn of all creation (the Son). This Son receives his being entirely from the Father in a relationship of utter submission and love. So Jesus does not exist through himself; he is entirely from the Father, who gives to him all that he is. He is thus a reflection of the Father, 'like the Father', receiving everything from the Father. The concept of the 'Word', developed in classical Greek thought, helps illuminate this Father-Son relationship within God. The Word is brought forth from the Intelligence to express its nature; the Word is distinct from the Intelligence and at the same time manifests it. And it is the Word which, in Jesus Christ, becomes flesh, human.

3. Through the Word in the Spirit

So the Father 'begets' the Word-Son and through him creates the world, because God's Word has creative power, bringing forth everything that is. The whole creation thus bears the mark of this Word of the Father and can be a source for the knowledge of God (as the early Fathers of the Church taught, speaking of 'seeds of the Word'). This creation finds its fulfilment in human beings, created by God in his image and according to his likeness (Genesis 1:26). Human beings attain wholeness by the rediscovery of this likeness to God, with the way to this goal being opened up by the Word that has become human. Through Jesus, humanity can enter into a right relationship with the Father, the source of Jesus' life. This 'righteousness', God's setting right of human beings with himself, is the work of the Holy Spirit in us (as in Jesus). The Spirit of God's love makes it possible for us to become children of the Father and brothers and sisters of the Son, the relationships for which we are destined in and through the Word of God. The Apostle Paul tells us that through the Holy Spirit we can call God 'Abba' (Galatians 4:6). We are thus 'God's children by adoption'. We live 'with, through and in Jesus' (the doxology of the Eucharistic Prayer).

4. Father – Son – Spirit

A second distinction within God thus becomes apparent. Already in the Old Testament there was mention by name of the Spirit, designating the creative power of God, the divine breath of life (*ruah* in Hebrew, *rûh* in Arabic). This same Spirit inspired the prophets and led the people of Israel, directed the mind of the people towards the knowledge of the true God and guided their history so that they might submit to God's will. Through the Spirit the Creator remains in a living relationship with his creation and the creation remains open to the activity of the Creator. Jesus confirms this revelation, above all in his own person, since he is 'conceived by the Holy Spirit', who unites in him divinity and humanity. In the Spirit Jesus is the 'Son' of God, and it is the Spirit (especially in Luke's Gospel) who is the source of his activity. But Jesus also tells us that this Spirit is the one who establishes the communion which binds him to the Father and makes them one. This very relationship, however, must necessarily be divine: only God can bring unity with God.

49

This Spirit is therefore of the same nature as the Father and the Son: he is divine. He is the bond of communion within God's very self, the principle of God's unity. As the reciprocal love between the Father and the Son, he is not only a divine attribute, but truly God. Hence the ancient practice, among the first Christians, of offering prayer 'to the Father, through the Son, in the Spirit'. We turn to the source of our life through Jesus, whom we follow, in the Spirit, whom he gives to us at baptism and who binds us back to the Father as his 'adopted' children.

5. Communion in Love

The Spirit is therefore the 'inner law' leading Christians on God's way. He brought life to Jesus and brings life to us also. The whole creation is thus called to enter into the loving communion which God is in God's very self. The Spirit is given to human beings to enable them to be the free and creative agents of the universal reconciliation which is the work of God and humanity in co-operation. Unity is indeed the source and the goal of the whole work of God, for unity is in God's very self. What distinguishes Christians from Muslims, however, is that they believe that this unity is communion, in a relationship of love.

> In her task of fostering unity and love among men, and even among nations, [the Church] gives primary consideration ... to what human beings have in common and to what promotes fellowship among them. For all peoples comprise a single community, and have a single origin, since God made the whole race of men dwell over the entire face of the earth (cf. Acts 17:26). One also is their final goal: God. His providence, His manifestations of goodness, and His saving designs extend to all men (cf. Wisdom 8:1; Acts 14:17; Romans 2:6-7; 1 Timothy 2:4) against the day when the elect will be united.[23]

6. Trinity

The triunity of God is fundamental to the Christian faith, drawing us away from the allure of idols, which are not God, and directing us towards the worship of the one and only, true and living God. More than that, it is the source of the unity of the human race, which is called to enter into the divine fellowship through the Holy Spirit.

> If you love me, you will keep my commandments. And I will ask the Father, and he will give you another Advocate, to be with you forever. This is the Spirit of truth, whom the world cannot receive, because it neither sees him nor knows him. You know him, because he abides with you, and he will be in you. I will not leave you orphaned; I am coming to you . . . On that day you will know that I am in my Father, and you in me . . . Those who love me will keep my word, and my Father will love them, and we will come to them and make our home with them' (John 14:15-18,20,23).

Through baptism, and in the Spirit, Christians have become members of the Body of Christ. In this Body they continue the mission of Jesus to liberate the human race from the imprisoning powers of death. Having been received into his Body they enter into eternal life, which is a sharing in God's own life. They receive this gift (which is Jesus himself) and strive to live by it. They seek to persevere in adoration of the divine mystery and to be guided by the Holy Spirit.

'Now to him who by the power at work within us is able to accomplish abundantly far more than all we can ask or imagine, to him be glory in the Church and in Christ Jesus to all generations, forever and ever' (Ephesians 3:20-21).

7.   The origin of the doctrine of the Trinity

It is important to draw attention to the origins of this doctrine. In this context a distinction can be drawn between the content of the doctrine and its cultural clothing.

i.   Jesus belongs to Israel, the chosen people. His thinking is entirely permeated by the spirit of a thoroughgoing monotheism (Mark 12:28-34). The Bible speaks repeatedly of the jealousy of the one and only God with regard to false gods. Jesus does not say that he is God but calls himself

'God's Son' (John 10:36), or simply 'the Son' (cf. Matthew 11:27). Jesus points to his 'heavenly' origin precisely by using the title 'Son of Man', which he takes from the vision of Daniel (Daniel 7). What is fundamental is that Jesus lives in a distinct relationship to God, whom he dares to call 'Abba' (Father, or even 'Daddy'). The titles 'Son of God' and 'Messiah' were, on their own, too vague in the time of Jesus to be able to communicate his view of himself. Jesus spoke only rarely of the Holy Spirit, but his life is nevertheless lived entirely in the power of the Spirit.

ii.   It is only after the Passion and Resurrection of Jesus that the disciples, through the powerful inspiration of the Spirit, understand the meaning of what they have experienced with Jesus. They then come to recognize that this Christ (Messiah), living, risen from the dead, is identical with Jesus of Nazareth, with whom they have lived and whom they have seen dying on the cross. They dare to confess that he is Saviour and Lord, and that in his relationship to his Father he is in a quite unique sense the Son of God. So now the 'trinitarian formulae' become more frequent, the title 'Son of God' is used, and there is also talk of the 'Spirit of God' (*pneuma* in Greek, the divine breath), whose presence the apostles have experienced so powerfully, even before they have given him a precise name. We thus come to the central confession of the Christian faith, that God is Father, Son and Spirit. This confession owes its existence to the reality of the risen Jesus and is rooted in the faith of the apostles.

iii. Because of the extremely numerous christological heresies of the 3rd and 4th centuries, it became necessary to strengthen faith in both the unity of God and also in the reality of the Father, Son and Spirit. A gradually maturing process led finally to the formula of the 4th Lateran Council in 1215, which explains that there are distinctions between the persons but unity in nature. The Father is the unoriginated origin, the Son owes his origin to the Father from all eternity, and the Spirit proceeds from both. Thus, the Father, the Son and the Holy Spirit are of one substance.[24]

Christian Answers

1. Christians unambiguously confess faith in the one God. Classical Christian theology affirms that in relating to the creation the creator acts as the one and only God.

2. The 'threeness' relates both to God's saving acts in history and also to God's inner life. It does not undermine his unity in any way. Mathematical categories are not capable of grasping the reality of God.[25] One and the same God is Father, Son and Spirit. In Jesus Christ God has become truly human. Suffering and death thus do not leave God unaffected. These divine names belong to the very core of the Christian faith and represent a part of its inheritance which has been passed on from the earliest stages. However, these concepts are not to be understood in the sense of an act of begetting by God, in the human sense of the word begetting. We agree absolutely with Muslims in our firm rejection of such an idea.[26] The refusal of Muslims to apply the concept of Fatherhood to God can help Christians to remain conscious of the metaphorical character of all language about God. Even for the Christian faith, God remains ineffable, beyond human speech. In other words, the terms 'Father' and 'Son' are used in a much wider sense by Christians than by Muslims. The one God is called 'Father' because he is the source of all being; he is called 'Son' because in Jesus he lives entirely from this source; he is called 'Spirit' because he communicates himself to his creation. God, the One, perfect and complete in himself, exalted, is in his very self love, interpersonal exchange, loving mutuality of giving and receiving. He is God in three persons, the triune God.

3. Where questions are raised about the meaning of the terms 'nature' and 'person', clarification should be sought from the historical context, making reference particularly to the distinction between the modern understanding of personhood and that of the classical philosophical and theological tradition.

4. God exists in three distinct modes of being (*ahwâl*), both in his relationship to us and in the relationships between the divine persons.[27]

5. Some medieval Christian theologians writing in Arabic favoured the use of certain metaphors in their attempts to explain the doctrine of the Trinity with Muslim questions in mind. So, for example, they pointed to how fire contains flame, heat and light, and to the three forms of ice, water and steam in which the same element appears.

6. It is worth considering the ninety-nine 'most beautiful names [i.e., of God]' (*al-asmâ' al-husnâ*), which play an important role in Islamic spirituality and theology. These names (e.g. 'the Almighty', 'the Compassionate', 'the All-Knowing', 'the Victorious', 'the Avenger') give expression in Islamic piety and theology to the abundant richness of God's being; in Muslim understanding, however, they of course do not jeopardize God's unity. When reflecting upon these divine names in the context of explaining the Christian teaching on the Holy Trinity one should keep in mind two points. Firstly, the 'persons' of the Trinity, strictly speaking, do not belong to the same category as the 'most beautiful names'. The divine names and attributes in Islamic understanding describe aspects of the divine 'nature', while each of the three 'persons' in the understanding of the Christian faith is fully God and therefore can be described by all the divine names, with the possible exception of certain names which Christians might not wish to apply to God. It is therefore not possible to use the divine names to distinguish the divine 'persons'. Secondly, Muslims will ask why Christians only emphasize 'three' names for God, when there are in fact many more 'most beautiful names' for God. Here the point made above applies again. For Christians, there are indeed many attributes that can be predicated of God; Christians may in fact include attributes other than those listed in the 'most beautiful names' identified by Muslims. But as regards divine 'persons', God has revealed himself as Father, Son and Holy Spirit, so Christians speak of 'Three-in-One', Trinity.

Chapter 6

The Church

I. Muslim Questions

▶ How far can we compare the Church and the *Umma* (the community of Muslims) and at what points do they differ?

▶ What are the main differences between the various Christian churches?

▶ Is there a search for unity among Christians?

▶ How does somebody become a member of the Church? What is the meaning of baptism?

▶ How is the Church governed? Is there a body corresponding to the mosque committee?

▶ What is the understanding in the Catholic Church of the role of the Pope, his infallibility, the teaching office of the Church and the Vatican State? Does 'infallibility' correspond to the Islamic concept of *i 'sâm* (*ma 'sûm* in adjectival form), which indicates being protected from sins?

II. Muslim Perspectives

General

1. Muslims understand themselves as members of the *Umma*, the community of Muslims, who in God's sight are all alike.

There is here fundamentally no hierarchy, no teaching office with authority on questions of faith, no priesthood and no clergy. Every single Muslim stands directly before God without any mediator.

2. In the consciousness of Muslims the unity of the *Umma* overrides the different groups within Islam (e.g., Sunnis and Shi'ites) and also the division of the Muslim world into different independent states, even when these are sometimes in conflict or at war with each other. In contrast, Christians appear to be divided into different groups, and not only within the Islamic world.

3. In the consciousness of the Muslim the interpretation of the Qur'an and the tradition are fundamentally responsibilities of the individual believer. The system of *ijmâ'* (the consensus of religious scholars) no longer applies. There are certainly Muslims who long for a teaching office which could protect the unity of the faith and expound the faith in today's world. More frequently, however, one encounters great doubt over the idea of a binding authority in matters of faith.

4. Generally speaking, people are Muslims because they were born in a Muslim country and grew up in the context of Islamic faith. The same is assumed about Christians. Furthermore, the essential difference between Christian baptism and Islamic circumcision is not often clearly understood. Arabic Muslims will sometimes translate the Arabic word for circumcision as 'baptism'. On the other hand, there are increasing numbers of both Muslims and Christians who consciously convert to their faith as adults or commit themselves to it afresh.

Detailed

1. Within the *Umma* all believers (whether men or women) are of equal value in God's eyes, 'like the teeth of a comb' (Hadith). 'The most honoured among you in the sight of Allah is (he who is) the most righteous among you' (Qur'an 49:13). Devotion to God does not require a mediator, even if most

Muslims in fact accord great significance to the intercession of saints. It is generally believed by Muslims that Muhammad is a living intercessor for them at the throne of God, though Wahhabi Muslims[28] emphasize, with reference to different Qur'anic verses, that this intercession only takes place on the Last Day and with God's express permission (see 2:256 and 20:108, among other texts).

2. The *Umma* is the community of all believers: 'the believers are but a single brotherhood' (49:10). It is the duty of the Caliph (in the past) and the head of state (today) to concern themselves about the cohesion of the *Umma* and to ensure that Muslim Law is upheld, although it is not normally their function to provide detailed definition and interpretation of the faith and the Law.

3. Defining what Muslims should believe and how they should practise their faith is the responsibility of the religious scholars (*'ulamâ'*, those with good knowledge of the religious sciences; *fuqahâ'*, those who have studied *fiqh*, the religious Law). The community, namely, the *Umma* as a whole, is infallible as regards the definition of the faith and the Law: 'My community will never agree in error' (Hadith). The outworking of this principle is, however, very difficult. In individual countries a grand mufti or a board of muftis (*dâr al-iftâ'*) are responsible for the official interpretation of the Law through formal legal decisions, known as fatwas. A Muslim can also seek advice from scholars and/or from spiritual leaders (*'ulamâ'* and Sufi sheikhs) who are recognized for their competence and experience.

4. It is the role of the *imâm* to preside over the ritual prayer (*salât*) and to deliver the sermon (*khutba*). He is normally a public official, paid by the Government. In his absence, his place can be taken by any competent Muslim male. The *imâm* is not a priest. There is no clergy in Islam, but rather scholars with a good knowledge of the religious sciences.

5. There are many movements in Islam all claiming to be the true way. Nevertheless, many Muslims today take the view

that the division between Sunnis and Shi'ites in particular, not to mention the divisions between smaller groups and theological schools, is a historical matter, and that the various movements all emphasize different aspects of Islam, each of them rooted in the Qur'an.

6. Christianity appears to Muslims to be more divided than Islam, not least in view of Christian teaching about the nature and significance of Jesus Christ. When the Qur'an mentions Jesus or Christians, it often draws attention to disunity among Christians:

'But the sects differ among themselves: and woe to the unbelievers because of the (coming) judgement of a momentous Day!' (19:37; cf. 2:113,145; 5:14.)

For Muslims in Europe this applies particularly to the division of Christians into Catholics and Protestants.

III. Christian Perspectives

1. Catholic/Protestant.[29]

i. In Christian understanding, 'Church' is a multi-layered concept. It is first of all the community of those who believe in Jesus as Son of God and Saviour and confess him in baptism. This broad community of the baptized is divided into different Christian churches.

ii. One becomes a Christian not by birth but through faith and baptism.[30] The one who is baptized is united with the death and Resurrection of Jesus (Romans 6) and thus becomes a member of the Church.

iii. The Church constantly strives to be faithful to the word of God in the Old and New Testaments and to understand it in the context of each new era. The Holy Spirit, whom Jesus promised to his disciples, is active in this continuing renewal in the understanding of the word of God, as it is worked out in the community of the Church.

1.1 Distinctive Protestant Beliefs

The Church exists where the word of God is truly proclaimed and the sacraments of baptism and the Lord's Supper are administered in keeping with the Gospel.[31] The Church is based on local congregations. Its constitution is synodical; its leaders, whether ministers or bishops, are accountable to synodical boards, composed of ordained and lay members. All leadership in the Church, whether exercised by men or women, married or single, is understood as a form of service between brothers and sisters.

1.2 Distinctive Catholic Beliefs

First and foremost, the Church is the People of God, in which all people are of equal value on the basis of their baptism. The purpose of ordained ministry within the Church is to serve the community of believers. The 2nd Vatican Council, in its Constitution on the Church (*Lumen Gentium*), deliberately speaks of a 'hierarchical community' (*communio hierarchica*).[32] The Church is not the hierarchy but rather the community of Christians; the hierarchy serves the community.

To understand correctly the doctrine of the 'infallibility'[33] of the pope and of the bishops, one must above all note that it is fundamentally the word of God communicated in Jesus Christ that is infallible, i.e., entirely reliable and free of error. Jesus proclaims and bears witness to the truth about God (cf. John 18:37). This truth is disclosed to the Church through the work of the Holy Spirit and it is received by the Church in faith. The Holy Spirit, the 'Spirit of truth', leads the disciples of Jesus into the whole truth (John 16:13). In the faith of the Church, brought about by the Spirit, there is the certainty of divine truth. Thus the 2nd Vatican Council explains: 'The body of the faithful as a whole, anointed as they are by the Holy One (cf. 1 John 2:20,27), cannot err in matters of belief'.[34]

This freedom from error is given when the believers as a whole express 'universal agreement in matters of faith and morals' (Ibid.). The infallibility in matters of faith which belongs to the

Church as a whole takes concrete form in the fellowship of the bishops as successors of the apostles (above all in an ecumenical council) and in the ministry of the one who, as the Apostle Peter's successor, is charged with the ministry of unity in the Church (the papal office). Infallibility thus does not belong to the pope as a private individual, nor are all his doctrinal statements infallible. Infallibility is ascribed to his doctrinal decisions when he is speaking *ex cathedra*, i.e., when, by virtue of his office as 'supreme shepherd and teacher of all the faithful . . . he proclaims by a definitive act some doctrine of faith or morals'.[35] So the pope, and equally the community of bishops, cannot arbitrarily declare certain teachings infallible; rather, they are bound to the beliefs to which the Church as a whole is committed and which it passes on. Hence, before a doctrinal decision is made, they must attend to the witness to the faith in the Scriptures, in the tradition of the Church and in the living experience of faith of Christian believers ('*sensus fidei*').[36]

Conversely, it is just as necessary for the community of believers to hear the faith proclaimed reliably and authoritatively. Such reliable proclamation is the task of the ordained ministry in the Church, which is rooted in the mission of the apostles and – specifically for the office of Peter – in the mission which Jesus entrusted to Peter (cf. Matthew 16:18; Luke 22:32; John 21:15-17).

The universal Church, as it is understood and as it takes form in the Catholic Church, is a fellowship of local churches of equal status. The unity of the local churches is grounded in the diocese, led by a bishop. The diocese is divided into parishes, which are entrusted by the bishop to parish priests.[37] Responsibility for the local churches lies with the bishop, who sends out priests, as his fellow-workers, to bring together a group of believers in a congregation. It is the priest's task, supported as far as possible by other office-holders in the church, to gather together the Christians in the name of Christ, to preside at celebrations of the Eucharist, to celebrate the other sacraments and to be responsible for the teaching and pastoral care of the believers. The totality of dioceses or local churches constitutes the universal Church. The guidance of the universal Church, and the maintenance of its unity, are the tasks of the Bishop of Rome, the Pope, as successor of the Apostle Peter, together with the College of Bishops.

The leaders of the Eastern Churches, whether independent of the Pope in Rome or united with him (the 'Uniate' Churches), are known as Patriarchs.

2. The Churches and the Unity of the Church

Practically from its very beginnings the Church has known the pain of schisms (divisions) and heresies (serious departures from correct belief). Alongside theological issues, political and moral factors have played an important or even decisive role.[38] In the world today there are three main branches of Christendom that have spread across the whole world: Catholicism, Protestantism and Orthodoxy.[39] For several centuries they have lived in opposition to each other, at times in armed conflict. They have also often engaged in sharp competition with each other in mission-fields, not always with great honesty. This contradicts the message of Jesus and his prayer for unity (John 17).

In the early decades of the 20th century the ecumenical movement, which works for the unity of the Church, saw considerable progress. 1948 saw the foundation of the World Council of Churches (WCC), to which most Protestant Churches, the Anglican Church and most of the Orthodox Churches belong. The Catholic Church, which reckons more than half the world's Christians as members and so is in numerical terms by far the strongest Christian Church, has not joined the WCC, even after the 2nd Vatican Council. However, it takes part in the work of the main WCC commissions and has achieved important agreements with its different member churches on the Eucharist, ministry, authority in the Church and the role of the Pope. The way towards the unity of Christians is therefore open; the goal is that all Christians should recognize each other as brothers and sisters in Christ, that they should listen to each other and, wherever and however possible, that they should work together.

IV. Christian Answers[40]

1. The Church and the *Umma* are both communities of believers. They both also encompass social and worldly dimensions. The *Umma* understands itself as commissioned to take forward the work of Muhammad in the contemporary world by bringing about the recognition of God's will. To the *Umma* as comprehensive community there corresponds the Church as spiritual unity and visible representation of Christ and of his kingdom. The Catholic Church is more strongly characterized by hierarchical structure and official teaching, while in the Protestant churches the synodical principle is more strongly stressed, even where structures of leadership have been thoroughly developed. The two emphases must not be considered mutually exclusive.

2. Papacy and Caliphate. As a head of state, the caliph was a worldly ruler; the authority of the Pope today is of a purely spiritual nature. The tiny contemporary Vatican State ensures the political independence of the Pope and the Curia, i.e., the central organ of the Catholic Church. The nuncios or envoys of the Pope are not the messengers of a worldly ruler; they are essentially no more than the personal representatives of a spiritual leader.[41]

3. Infallibility in the Catholic Church[42] and in the *Umma*. The fundamental principle is present in both the Catholic Church and the *Umma*. The common factor is that infallibility essentially belongs to the community of believers; the difference lies in how it is determined.[43] In Catholic understanding there is a need for a teaching office, guided by the Holy Spirit, so that along with the inevitable developments which unfold over the generations the Church might be kept faithful to the Gospel.

4. The Catholic priest and the Protestant minister, like the imam, preside over the liturgical prayers, preach and teach. The Catholic priest and the Protestant minister are ordained. In contrast, the imam is a Muslim commissioned by a mosque congregation or an organisation of mosques to preside over

a congregation of Muslims. To work as an imam it is not
necessary to undergo vocational theological training.

5. Baptism, confession of faith and circumcision. A person is
a Muslim through being born to Muslim parents or through
conversion to Islam by reciting the *shahâda*, the confession
of faith, before witnesses. A person becomes a member of
the Christian Church through baptism, which includes the
confession of faith in Jesus as the Son of God. Circumcision,
which is not mentioned in the Qur'ân, is only *sunna* (i.e., a
tradition based on Hadîth). For some legal scholars it is
compulsory; for others it is recommended. It applies to boys;
some also wish to apply it to girls, but this is rejected by
most Muslims.[44]

6. Unity in the Church and in the *Umma*. Both Church and
Umma have experienced schisms and rivalries, often
accompanied by bloodshed. Human factors, errors and sins
should not be denied or glossed over. Within the Church this
might mean, for example, public acknowledgment by the
Catholic Church of the ways it contributed to the schism
with the Eastern Church and to the divisions of the Church
in the 16th century, and likewise acknowledgement by
Protestant churches of the conflicts among themselves. This
offers the opportunity to explain that according to the Catholic
faith the Christian Church is at the same time of divine and
human, that is fallible, nature; and that, for both Catholics
and Protestants the Church is at the same time holy and yet
composed of sinners. The recognition that the Church is in a
continuous process of reform[45] implies the constant
challenge to engage in fresh thinking within the Church, but
this should not be misunderstood as an invitation to bring
about further division. Just as Muslims feel that despite the
division of Islam into various branches they are brothers in
the faith, Christians should also recognize, across
confessional boundaries, that they are one in Christ and are
called to work together wherever possible: in the translation
and interpretation of the Bible; in theological reflection and
research; in the development of spirituality and witness; in
social and in charitable work.

Chapter 7

The Holy Eucharist

I. Muslim Questions

▶ How do you pray? How do you perform your Christian prayers (*salât, namâz*)? Why do you pray with bread and wine (or, what is this white disk and what is this cup)? You pray with wine! *Harâm*! In his Law God forbids the drinking of wine.

▶ Do you really believe that God is present in this bread and wine? That bread and wine become God himself? You 'eat' God?

▶ What is in that box on or behind the altar? Why do you leave a lamp burning by the altar? What is the difference between the celebration of the Eucharist in a large church on Sunday and on weekdays in a smaller church or chapel?

II. Muslim Perspectives

General

1. Ritual prayer (*salat*) involves adopting a sequence of physical positions and reciting prayers for which the exact wording is prescribed. This is distinct from spontaneous prayers of petition (*du'a*), for which there are no prescribed wordings or rituals.

2. The emphasis on the transcendence of God leads to a firm rejection of any idea of the indwelling of God (*hulûl*[46]) in what he has created, especially in inanimate objects such as bread and wine. The use of wine presents a particular scandal as it has been utterly forbidden in Islam from the time of the Qur'an onwards.

3. There is a mistaken, indeed a quite wrong way of conceptualizing and expressing the Eucharist, developed and spread by a particular Christian tradition, which Muslims understandably reject: i.e., the mistaken doctrine of 'impanation' (God becoming bread), which holds that 'This bread is Jesus (or God)'. This error is strengthened by a false understanding of the doctrine of 'Transubstantiation'. 'Substance' is today generally understood to refer to an object as it is experienced in its concrete and material aspect. Within this way of thinking, a change of the 'substance' of the bread into the body of Christ is simply nonsense, for the physical material of the bread remains unchanged in the Eucharist. On these assumptions, the Catholic doctrine of Transubstantiation is understandably rejected. To understand this doctrine correctly, however, one must grasp that 'substance' means the metaphysical reality of the bread. All reality that can be physically experienced is understood within the category of 'accident' or 'species'; and within this category of 'accident' no alteration or transformation occurs to the bread during the Eucharist. This is exactly what the doctrine of Transubstantiation seeks to maintain. 'Magical' understandings of the sacrament, along with the idea that the words of the priest have the power automatically to change something into something else, are to be firmly rejected.

Detailed

1. The Qur'an and the whole Muslim tradition describe Christians as people who pray, whatever their doctrinal errors might be. This applies especially to monasticism (*rahbâniyya*), a word indicating all men and women who

dedicate themselves chiefly to prayer (cf. Qur'an 5:82; 24:36-37,57).

> Strongest among men in enmity to the believers you will find the Jews and pagans; and nearest among them in love you will find those who say, "We are Christians", because among these are priests and monks, and they are not arrogant (5:82).

2. At the time of the Qur'an and in the early centuries of Islamic history, Christian hermitages and monasteries represented an integral part of the traditional landscape in many areas within the Muslim world. Indeed in Islamic societies churches, the clergy and Christian worship were protected by a special law.

3. In sura *al-mâ'ida*, the Qur'an contains an unmistakeable allusion to the Eucharist:

> Behold! The disciples said: "O Jesus, son of Mary, can your Lord send down to us a table from heaven?" Jesus said: "Fear Allah, if you are believers." They said: "We only wish to eat of it and satisfy our hearts, and to know that you have indeed told us the truth and that we ourselves may be witnesses of it." Jesus, the son of Mary, said: "O Allah our Lord! Send down to us a table from heaven, that there may be for us – the first and the last of us – a festival and a sign from you; and provide for our sustenance, for you are the best sustainer." Allah said: "I will send it down to you; but if any of you after that resists faith I will punish him with a penalty such as I have not inflicted on anyone among all the peoples" (5:112-115).

Although some commentators on the Qur'an see in this passage allusions to the multiplication of loaves (Mark 6:30-44 and parallels) and/or to the vision of Peter at Joppa, when he sees a linen sheet filled with ritually unclean animals let down onto the earth and he is commanded to eat (Acts 10:9ff.), all recognize that the main allusion here is to the Eucharist. The apostles ask Jesus to bring down from heaven a *mâ'ida*, a table spread for a meal, to convince them that he has truly been sent by God. Then Jesus himself makes this request to God, and God promises to fulfil the request. The passage states that the *mâ'ida* is a gift from heaven (v.112) and that it will be a festival (the Arabic term *'id* indicates a regularly recurring festival, possibly alluding to Easter and to every Sunday), a festival to the end of time ('for the first and the last'); it will also bring 'deep peace' (*tuma'nîna* v.113) to the hearts of those who share in it; they must 'bear witness about it' (v.113), while those who are unbelieving after they have received this *mâ'ida* will be punished severely (cf. 1 Corinthians 11:27-32).

III. Christian Perspectives

From earliest times, the Eucharist has been at the heart of the Church's worship. In it is celebrated the memory of the life, death and Resurrection of Jesus Christ. Christians believe that Jesus Christ is alive as the one raised from the dead by God and so he remains always present with the Church: 'And remember, I am with you always, to the end of the age' (Matthew 28:20). At its celebrations of the Eucharist the Christian congregation gathers together and knows Jesus Christ to be present in their midst – according to the saying of Jesus that has been passed down: 'For where two or three are gathered in my name, I am there among them' (Matthew 18:20). The congregation prays and hears God's word, as it is communicated in Scripture; here also Christ, the Word of God, is present.

Then the congregation performs what the New Testament accounts tell us Jesus did at his last meal, on the evening before he suffered: over bread and the cup of wine he uttered the prayers of thanksgiving and blessing and then in the broken bread and in the outpoured wine he gave himself to the disciples. In the blessed gifts of bread and wine Jesus shares his very self as the one who offers himself up so that human beings might be redeemed and set free from sin and guilt. Whenever the Christian congregation is gathered for the Eucharist (thanksgiving), it celebrates the memory of this self-offering or sacrifice, confident in the faith that Jesus is present and that when the prayers of thanksgiving and blessing are said over the bread and wine he gives himself to the believers as they receive this holy sacrament. Jesus introduces those who celebrate this memory and receive him in the gifts into his own trusting relationship with God, his Father, and into his self-offering for humanity. Thus those who celebrate the Eucharist together are transformed and taken into the 'Body of Christ'.

In all of this, the bread and wine remain unaltered in their concrete, physical, material reality; the 'form' (or *species*, to use the technical Latin term) of bread and wine is entirely preserved. But the bread and wine are taken into a new context, where they acquire a new significance and reality: in them the Jesus Christ who is alive in God gives his very self. Bread and wine thus gain an entirely new meaning, given by Jesus Christ himself and based in God himself. But because a reality ultimately *is* what it is before God, it is necessary to say that in the Eucharist bread and wine are transformed in their deepest reality: their deepest reality is now that they communicate the presence of Jesus Christ. This also clarifies what is meant by the Catholic doctrine of the Transubstantiation of the bread and wine, the transformation of their essence: bread and wine are transformed in their deepest reality (in their metaphysical 'substance' or their essence). Their deepest reality is no longer to provide nourishment and pleasure for the earthly lives of human beings, but rather to communicate the presence of Jesus as nourishment for eternal life (cf. John 6). Considered in their physical aspects, bread and wine remain unchanged; Jesus does not become bread and wine in their physical reality. So Jesus is not chewed when the bread is eaten; he does not restrict himself into the small space of the bread; he does not suffer when the bread is broken. Rather than expressing the Church's teaching on the Eucharist, such ideas contradict it.

IV. Christian Answers

1. In dialogue with Muslims who are familiar with the Qur'an, it is always good to make the story of *al-mâ'ida* one's starting-point.[47] As bidden by Jesus, we gather at this *mâ'ida*

or table, which Jesus has left behind him as a memorial of the end of his earthly life. The Christian can thus also mention the suffering and the death of Jesus on the cross, while being well aware that the Qur'an – as interpreted by virtually all Muslims – explicitly denies this death.

2. Bread and wine are used when the Eucharist is celebrated because Jesus himself used them at the Last Supper to express his self-offering. Among the people of Israel, bread and wine were basic forms of food and drink and the breaking of the bread and the blessing of the cup of wine were prominent and significant rituals at festival meals. What Jesus did at the Last Supper was thus linked to existing traditions. In faithfulness to its historical origins, the Church has also used bread and wine when celebrating the Eucharist. There have been some changes in the details of the eucharistic rituals and practices. Thus, instead of the bread that was broken and distributed at the festival, in due course use was made of wafers ('hosts') that could be broken up into smaller pieces; these, however, scarcely resembled bread. Today hosts are used which can more readily be seen as bread.

In Israel it was in general permitted to drink wine, which is seen as a gift from God, bringing joy to human hearts (Psalm 104:15). At the feast anticipated at the end of time, prepared for all people, there will be served the finest, choice wines (Isaiah 25:6). In the Eucharist there is a living hope for this fulfilment at the end of time in the Kingdom of God; here also, therefore, the fruit of the vine is drunk (cf. Matthew 14:25). For wine to be obtained, however, the grapes must first be trampled in the wine-press (cf. Isaiah 16:10). Thus it is that the cup of wine from which we drink at the Eucharist speaks of the life of Jesus offered for human beings. This self-offering, and in it the reconciling love of God, the outpouring of divine life, are given to the believer in the Eucharist (communion). This spiritual nourishment is the meaning of the Eucharist.

3. Belief in the presence of Jesus Christ in the Eucharist is closely connected with belief in God's becoming human in

Jesus Christ (the Incarnation). In the humanity of Jesus, and in his sacrifice on behalf of many, God is present in the world and reveals himself unreservedly and definitively as reconciling love. 'God was in Christ, reconciling the world to himself' (2 Corinthians 5:19). The life of Jesus is a life entirely in God and through his dying he was taken up into the life of God (Resurrection, glorification). Living in God, he is present to the world. We can therefore meet him, pray to him and listen to him everywhere. However, there are distinct ways in which he communicates his presence (just as a person can show his presence to another in distinct ways: through speech, gestures and actions or even through a pregnant silence). The Eucharist is an especially significant and privileged way through which Christ is present: he communicates himself in the concrete, visible gifts of bread and wine in order to establish a deep and inward spiritual communion with and between believers. This communion is the source of the Church's life.

4. The bread and wine over which the prayers of thanksgiving and blessing are spoken at a celebration of the Eucharist, and in which Christ is believed to be present, are normally distributed to be eaten and drunk there and then. However, from the early days of the Church a portion of the blessed, consecrated bread has been preserved so that those who are unable to attend the service – the old, the sick, the disabled – might also be able to share in the celebration of the Eucharist. Since it is part of Catholic belief that Christ is present and remains present in the eucharistic bread, this is treated with reverence, even after the service. It is kept in a dignified place in a so called 'tabernacle' and this place is indicated by a burning light, such as an oil-lamp or a candle. Respect for the presence of Christ in the bread is shown through particular signs and gestures, such as bowing and genuflecting. This does not, however, mean that the consecrated bread itself is worshipped; the worship is directed to Christ himself. Such forms of eucharistic veneration must remain closely tied to the actual celebration of the Eucharist, with its prayers of thanksgiving and blessing

and the receiving of communion in the gathered congregation.

5. The Eucharist and all other liturgical services can be celebrated in places of various types and sizes, such as churches, chapels, large halls and so on. On Sundays, however, Christians are called, as far as possible, to gather for the celebration of the Eucharist in the local parish church.

Chapter 8

Prayer

I. Muslim Questions

▶ How do you pray? Where and when do you pray? How many times daily?

▶ Do you wash yourselves ritually before praying?

▶ Do women also pray?

▶ Do you pray at all times, or only on particular occasions?

▶ Do you have particular prayers for the major religious festivals?

▶ In what language do you pray?

▶ What are the main physical positions adopted in prayer? What does the sign of the cross mean?

▶ Why do you pray? Because God has commanded you to? Out of respect for religious rules? To gain entry to Heaven? Because it makes you feel better?

▶ What do you say in your prayers? What texts do you use? The Bible?

▶ Whom do you pray for? Can you pray for us?

▶ Can we take part in your prayers? Can we pray together? If so, what texts should we use?

▶ Is it permissible for Muslim prayers to be said in a Christian place of worship?

▶ Is it possible to organize a Muslim prayer-room within a Christian building?

II. Muslim Perspectives

General

The words 'prayer' and 'pray' have a wide range of meanings and do not express quite the same ideas as their Islamic equivalents. The key Islamic concept to grasp here is *'ibâda*, suggesting both worship and servanthood; prayer, as an act of *'ibâda*, expresses the essential attitude of humble service of the servant before his or her Lord. Islam distinguishes further between *salât*, the daily ritual prayers to be performed at certain prescribed times, and various forms of free, personal or private prayer. Examples of the latter include: *du'a* (invocation, petition), *munâjât* (intimate dialogue with God) and *dhikr* (recollection of God in prayer). There is therefore a distinction between 'performing the prayers' and 'praying'. When a Muslim asks questions about prayer, he or she instinctively thinks of the prescribed canonical prayers (*salât*), which are public, often communal and are performed according to quite specific prescriptions. Every other form of prayer is of much less significance.

In contrast, Christians think of prayer primarily in terms of an attitude of spirit and heart; in their minds prayer is not tied to a particular ritual form. Thus, when Muslims say 'I do not pray', they mean 'I do not regularly perform the prescribed ritual prayers'. It can nevertheless certainly be the case that God is often in the thoughts of such Muslims and frequently comes to the surface in their conversations. When Christians pray according to traditional monastic patterns ('praying the hours') this resembles Muslim prayer (*salât*) in its observance of a prescribed liturgy at set times. In Islam it is in the devotional life of mysticism and in the ways of prayer of the religious brotherhoods that one finds deeper prayer, meditation and wider understandings of prayer as spiritual, inward and wordless.

Christians do not practise regular ritual prayer in the same way as Muslims practise *salât*. It therefore seems clear that people in 'the West' do not pray, because their attitudes are 'materialistic'. In contrast, Muslims pray regularly, in public, and without any fear of what people will say, thus demonstrating that they belong to the Muslim community. Muslim consciousness of the transcendence of God brings to ritual prayer in Islam a sense of awe before the sacred. Vital importance is thus attached to the precise observance of the detailed ritual prescriptions concerning matters such as washing, bodily postures and ways of speaking (aloud, quietly or inwardly). In Christianity the feeling that 'God lives among us' has led to a certain familiarity in relationship to God, and to a freedom of style which goes so far that it can be interpreted as lacking in reverence for God.

To summarize, one can say that while Islam ascribes great significance to the outward form of prayer, Christianity puts great emphasis on the inward practice of prayer.

Detailed

In Islam the word 'prayer' indicates specific religious practices.

1. The 'canonical' ritual prayer (*salât*)

Salât, the second pillar of Islam, means ritual prayer and is an essential component of Muslim worship. When praying, the Muslim is in solidarity with fellow-believers around the world, across continents and cultures and also across the ages, and through ritual prayer experiences fellowship with other Muslims, despite possible differences of opinion. Prayer brings together many different aspects of devotion to God such as recitation, listening, meditation and attentiveness to God's presence. Prayer consists firstly of praise and thanksgiving, then also the seeking of forgiveness and of God's blessing, and, as the occasion demands, mourning, intercession and so on. To ensure that ritual prayer, wherever and whenever it is performed, contains all these elements, its rite has been prescribed in detail. It is derived from the Qur'an and Hadith, and from the legal regulations which the schools of Law worked out on the basis of the Qur'an and Hadith.

Ritual prayer is performed five times every day, at prescribed times. Many Muslim calendars also contain minutely detailed timetables for the prayers, the times for which can, however, be adjusted as necessity demands. The times for prayer are: at break of day (*subh*); at noon (*zuhr*); in the afternoon (*'asr*); at sunset (*maghrib*); during the night (*'isha*). The primary function of the call to prayer (âdhân), which the *mu'adhdhin* proclaims from the minaret, is to make people aware of the exact time for prayer. The â*dhân* gives a distinct rhythm to the life of Muslim towns.

When possible, prayer is performed communally. The ideal place for prayer is the mosque. Those praying stand in rows behind the imam, who decides the rhythm of the prayer. Prayer can also be performed on one's own or in small groups outside the mosque, and in principle anywhere, so long as the place is ritually clean. The place of prayer can be indicated by a carpet, a cloth, clean paper on the floor or a circle of stones. In any case, when performing the ritual prayer one must face towards Mecca, as long as the direction can be established. The direction for prayer (*qibla*) is indicated in mosques by the *mihrâb*, the prayer niche pointing towards Mecca. The fact that all who are performing the prayer are facing towards the Kaaba in Mecca underlines the worldwide unity of the Muslim community. Before beginning ritual prayer one must carry out the prescribed ablutions (ritual acts of washing). Normally water is used, but if this is not to hand or available for use a symbolic act of cleansing with sand is performed. The Law distinguishes between the requirements to wash the whole of one's body (*ghusl*) and part of it (*wudû'*). *Ghusl* is necessary if a person is in a condition of 'greater impurity' (*janaba*). This is the case after sexual intercourse, including within marriage, or after contact with a corpse. *Wudû'* is necessary in the case of 'lesser impurity' (*hadath*), which applies after any excretion from the body (faeces, urine, pus and so on). In this case it is necessary to wash one's hands, mouth, nose, face, forearms, head, ears, throat and feet. One's clothes must also be clean, but most important of all is purity of heart. It is instructive to compare the Islamic regulations with similar regulations in the Old Testament (Exodus 30; Leviticus 18; Deuteronomy 21; 23).

After the ablutions the worshipper declares his or her intention (*niyya*) to pray. The prayer opens with the *takbîr,* the formula '*Allâhu akbar*' ('God is greater'). This is followed by the recitation of the opening sura of the Qur'an, the *Fâtiha.*[48] Every ritual act of prayer consists of 2 to 4 liturgical units, each called a *rak'a.* This consists of a time standing upright (*wuqûf*), bowing (*rukû'*), prostration (*sujûd*) and sitting on one's heels (*julûs*); each of these bodily postures is accompanied by a specific and suitable prayer. The prayer at break of day includes two *rak'a*-s, the prayer at sunset includes three, while the noon, afternoon and night prayers each consists of four *rak'a*-s. Ritual prayer includes the recitation of some short suras from the Qur'an, followed by greetings addressed to God (*tahiyyât*), the Prophet and all Muslim believers. These are followed by the confession of faith (*shahâda*) and prayers for blessing on Muhammad and Abraham. The whole ritual usually lasts no longer than 5 to 10 minutes, unless longer Qur'anic texts or intercessions are added.

Every week congregational prayers (*salât al-jum'a*) take place on Friday at noon. The ritual is the same as for the daily prayers, expanded by fuller *tahiyyât* and particularly by the sermon, delivered either by the imam or by another Muslim with the necessary ability. On the occasion of major festivals there are further special rituals, particularly at the two most important festivals: the festival of sacrifice, also known as the Great Festival ('*Îdul adha* or '*Îdul kabir*), and the festival of breaking the fast at the end of Ramadan, the month of fasting ('*Îdul fitr*). Special rituals also mark the festival of the birth of the Prophet (*al-mawlid al-nabawî*), '*Ashûra* and the nights of Ramadan. Mention should also be made of the impressive prayers used in the course of the major and minor pilgrimages.

Salât is above all an act of adoration, praise and gratitude towards God. It is performed out of obedience towards God's command. Spiritual writers such as Muhammad al-Ghazâli (1058-1111) emphasize the following attitudes as essential in approaching *salât*: purity of heart, attentiveness to God's presence, reverent fear of God (*taqwà*), hope, modesty and the honest desire to amend one's life.

There are also ritual prayers for particular occasions, such as prayers for rain, at the time of natural disasters and at the time of bereavement. Voluntary ritual prayers (*nawâfil*) are performed during Ramadan and at night (Qur'an 17:79).

2. Other prayers

Sufism and the Sufi brotherhoods (*tarîqa*, pl. *turuq*) have developed the practice of *dhikr* (the recollection of God), which essentially consists of mentioning and celebrating the name of God (cf. Qur'an 2:152; 3:41). The constant repetition of God's name, whether this is done alone or with others, essentially aims to achieve the total permeation of the believer's heart and mind with recollection of God's name. Traditionally, there are three stages to *dhikr*: the *dhikr* of the tongue (the simple oral recitation of God's name); the *dhikr* of the heart (as the heart is taken up into the rhythm of the recitation); and the *dhikr* of intimacy (*sirr*), in which the believer's whole body and soul vibrate with the recitation of God's name. Sufis and brotherhoods also engage regularly in meditation (*fikr* and *ta'ammul*), daily silent prayer (*wird*) and responsive litanies (*hizb*).

These forms of prayer are, likewise, all strictly regulated in terms of ritual and text. The texts are often very striking. Nothing, however, is left to personal initiative. The Sufi disciple (*murâd*) is asked to perform these rituals with great care under the direction of a Sufi guide (*shaikh, pîr*).

The recitation of the '99 most beautiful names of God' (Qur'an 20:8; 17:100) should also be mentioned. These names are recited meditatively by pious Muslims with the use of prayer-beads (*subha, tasbiha*).

It is also significant that in various contexts and in situations of distress Muslims meditate on Qur'anic texts and find strength through doing so.

Finally, there are countless spontaneous prayers, not least

the many invocations which Muslims – especially simple believers – utter on all possible occasions: praise (*al-hamdu lillâh* – 'God be praised'); surprise (*mâ shâ' Allâh* – 'whatever God wills' or 'as long as God wills'); prayers for forgiveness (*astaghfir Allâh* – 'I ask for God's forgiveness'); prayers for healing (*Allâh yashfî* – 'may God heal'); expressions of disapproval or indignation (*lâ hawla wa lâ quwwata illâ bi-llâh al-'azîm* – 'there is no power or strength other than with God').

Muslim theologians have at times engaged in intense discussions about whether petitionary prayer is compatible with Islamic Law and what value should be ascribed to it. Since God knows everything, no prayer can alter his almighty will. Nevertheless, there is agreement among Muslims that *du'a* is pleasing to God and therefore desirable. Has not God himself invited believers to address prayers of petition to him (cf. Qur'an 2:186; 22:12; 13:14) and has he not promised to hear them (2:186; 40:60)? God, mainstream Islam teaches, foresees all things from eternity and in his sovereign goodness he grants requests generously. The Mu'tazilites, with their tendency towards rationalism, were of the opinion that although petitionary prayer has no effect it is profitable as it forms in people an appropriate attitude towards God, the attitude of a poor servant (*'abd faqîr*). Petitionary prayer does not change God, but it does change people.

3. Prayer and action

The genuineness of prayer is demonstrated in one's relations with one's neighbour, especially in striving for righteousness and in care for the poor:

> It is not righteousness that you turn your faces towards East or West; but it is righteousness to believe in Allah and the Last Day, and the angels and the Book and the messengers; to spend of your substance out of love for him, for your kin, for orphans, for the needy, for the wayfarer, for those who ask, and for the ransom of slaves; to be steadfast in prayer and practise regular charity ... (Qur'an 2:177).

III. Christian Perspectives

Prayer means turning to God in response to his giving himself to humanity. This turning to God can happen and be expressed in many and various ways: oral prayer; meditation; music, with or without an accompanying text; physical movement, including dance; the arts, including paintings, altar-pieces, images of saints, the icons of the Orthodox Church[49], stained-glass windows and statues. One could also mention here appeals to the senses, for example through the use of incense, especially in Catholic and Orthodox churches, and the interior layout of churches. In what follows, however, the emphasis lies on prayers that make use of words, whether these are spoken aloud, quietly or inwardly.

The origins of Christian prayer lie in the prayer-life of Jesus, with its Jewish roots, and also in what he said about prayer.

1. Jesus prayed and taught us to pray

The Gospels often portray Jesus at prayer. Jesus loved to withdraw to pray alone. He sometimes spent the whole night in prayer, especially before major decisions or turning-points in his life. For example, at the beginning of his public ministry he withdrew into the desert to pray and fast; he also prayed before his Passion. He lived in continual unity with God the Father, inspired by the desire to be at one with his will. The roots of Jesus' life of prayer were deep in Judaism and in its Scriptures. He quotes from the Psalms, the prayer-book of the Scriptures, either directly or re-phrasing freely. He taught his disciples how to pray. Private prayer should be uncomplicated and unadorned and should always avoid empty words and phrases (cf. Matthew 6:5-7). In response to an explicit request from his disciples, he gives them the prayer beginning 'Our Father'. 'Father' because God loves us as his children; 'our' because every prayer, even private prayer, is prayed in communion with others. The invocation 'Our Father' is followed by three petitions concerning God and three petitions at the human level.

Before his sufferings, Jesus celebrated a last meal out of which, after Easter, there evolved the memorial of that meal in the Lord's Supper or Eucharist. This is the sacrament of the total self-offering of Jesus to the Father for the world's salvation and of the real presence – albeit invisible and immaterial – of the risen Christ among us. So Christian prayer, as it has been taught and shaped by Jesus, is above all adoration of the Father, praise, thanksgiving, self-offering, request for forgiveness, help and hope.

As with Islamic prayer, as Christians we distinguish between liturgical and private prayer. Very great importance is attached to private prayer. Prayer is a matter as much for women as for men. In the Catholic and Orthodox Churches, however, only men are ordained to preside at the Eucharist.

2. Liturgical prayer

Liturgical prayer is communal prayer with prescribed rituals and texts. The Eucharist (also known as the Holy Mass by Catholics) stands at the centre of Christian life and prayer. In the Catholic Church a priest always presides at the Eucharist. It can be celebrated every day and at whatever time is chosen. On Sunday, the day when Christians particularly call to mind the risen Lord, the Eucharist is conducted with special solemnity. In the Catholic Church the Sunday liturgy can also be celebrated on Saturday evening.

The Eucharist begins with the ministry of the word, i.e., readings from the Scriptures, which always include a passage from one of the four Gospels, followed by a sermon or homily and prayers of intercession. Then follow the preparation of the bread and wine; the Eucharistic Prayer, which includes the 'words of institution' (the words of Jesus at the Last Supper); the 'Our Father'; and the giving of communion, when believers receive Jesus Christ himself in the forms of bread and wine.

The Eucharist is thus the great prayer of thanksgiving (hence the term 'Eucharist', from the Greek for 'to give thanks'), the Christian congregation's great prayer of adoration and praise; the Eucharist also involves sharing in God's word and being united with Jesus Christ, who gives his real presence in bread

81

and wine and so strengthens believers for their journey through life.

Liturgical prayer according to traditional monastic patterns ('praying the hours') is of great importance for monastic communities and for priests, but less common among lay people. This involves a sequence of prayers and readings from the Bible and the Church Fathers and includes recitation of the Psalms, hymns, responses and intercessions. In monastic communities it is recited or sung seven times daily: in the morning, at noon, in the evening and during the night. It can also be prayed by individuals. Prayer is also of central importance in Protestant churches.

For Catholics the sacraments include confirmation, penance, marriage, holy orders (ordination to the Church's ministry) and the anointing of the sick, as well as baptism and Eucharist; these are administered in the context of liturgical ceremonies. In many places, and following local traditions, there are also liturgical prayers during pilgrimages, liturgical prayers for rain, for a good harvest, for a safe birth, etc.

3. Private prayer

'Private prayer' refers to the prayer of a person alone or of a group of people, such as, for example, family prayers in the evening. In terms of form it is free; indeed flexibility in terms of style is generally an essential characteristic of Christian prayer. Private and public prayer complement each other and are not in competition. Both are in accordance with the call of Jesus to pray without ceasing (Mark 13:33; Luke 18:1-8; 21:36; cf. Colossians 1:9; 1 Thessalonians 5:17; 2 Thessalonians 1:11).

In the context of private prayer, alongside prayers expressed in an entirely free style, use is also made of prayers of the Church such as the 'Our Father', the Psalms, the Ave Maria (among Catholics) and other prayers, aloud or in silence. This is the practice of many Christians, especially in the morning and evening, or when they visit a church or chapel. Many Catholics also pray the rosary, reciting the 'Our Father' and the

'Ave Maria' alternately, with the recitation of one of the 'mysteries' of the life of Jesus in the middle of the sequence. Many recite the rosary at least once a day.

Christians who wish to deepen their life of prayer give time every day, if possible, to meditation and contemplation. Standing, kneeling, sitting or lying down, in a holy place or at home, they concentrate in silence on God to become conscious of his presence and to hear his word. The constant practice of this kind of regular attentiveness and listening to the words of Scripture, which can be helped by certain methods of meditation, is an effective way to grow closer to God. According to Catholic belief this can, by God's grace, lead to the attainment of mystical gifts, whether in monastic seclusion or in the midst of everyday life. In addition, Christians who wish to follow Jesus with great devotion undertake spiritual exercises from time to time, in silence and in prayer, whether on one day every month or for one week every year.

4. To whom is prayer addressed?

Prayer is directed to God. We pray to him through the mediation of Jesus Christ in the Holy Spirit. The discussion in chapter 5 ('God, the Three in One') is relevant here. We pray in and with Jesus, in the power of the Holy Spirit, to God alone.

In the Catholic Church, the practice of asking the saints to pray for us is based on the assumption that they are intercessors for us with God.[50] The fundamental orientation of prayer towards God, who alone is worthy of worship, is maintained.

5. The meaning of prayer

The essential attitude underlying prayer is worship, thanksgiving and petition for help for oneself and for others. Through prayer we are guided to seek the will of God at every moment. It is a source of strength, of peace, of joy and of fruitfulness.

It is helpful to have set times of prayer. These times of prayer will unconsciously make other areas of life fruitful, until finally the whole of life becomes prayer. Conversely, a life of genuine self-giving will enrich our prayer. Prayer will thus permeate our joys and our cares. Prayer is not a way of escaping from life. Prayer enables a person to search for the signs of the presence of God in individual and communal experience of life and to seek God's will when faced with decisions. Prayer is strength for living; it influences our relationship both to ourself and to our neighbour, permeating our heart (cf. 1 Corinthians 13).

6. The many forms of Christian prayer

Over the centuries, Christian prayer has changed and has assumed very varied forms at different times and places, in keeping with the prevailing cultures of countless peoples. Adaptation to contemporary culture can cause tensions but is a necessary process, which can also lead to new forms of prayer. This is especially the case in Muslim countries, where Christians attempt to integrate the richness of spiritual experience of these people and to translate this into the language of prayer.

IV. Christian Answers

1. It is worth emphasizing again the point made above (in section II) that the words 'prayer' and 'pray' have different meanings in Christian and Islamic contexts.

2. One should only compare like with like. Thus, for example, it is appropriate to compare *salât* (Muslim liturgical prayer) with Christian liturgical prayer such as the Eucharist and praying the hours, giving consideration to their formal characteristics, positions for prayer and melodic chanting, as well as the daily and weekly cycles for prayer. Muslim petitionary prayer corresponds to Christian private prayer, especially prayers of supplication, while *dhikr* (recollection of God in prayer) corresponds to forms of Christian contemplation.

3. One should note the elements shared by Christian and Muslim prayer, such as:

- ♦ the same aims and meaning in prayer, such as worship and thanksgiving;
- ♦ similar daily and weekly patterns of prayer;
- ♦ similarity between texts; the Psalms, for example, are relatively accessible for Muslims;
- ♦ certain bodily positions.

4. One should avoid simplistic contrasts between the 'formality' of Muslim prayer and the 'inwardness' of Christian prayer. Naturally there are differences of emphasis, but it is of the essence of both these traditions of prayer that they have inward as well as outward dimensions. Outward liturgical form is important for Christians as well as for Muslims.

5. As regards the absence of ritual ablutions in Christian prayer, it should be noted that before the time of Jesus legal and cultic purity was as strictly prescribed in Jewish religion as it is in Islam today. In the tradition of the great prophets, Jesus opposed formalism and spoke of the link between genuine prayer and healthy human relationships.

'Do you not see that whatever goes into the mouth enters the stomach, and goes out into the sewer? But what comes out of the mouth proceeds from the heart, and this is what defiles. For out of the heart come evil intentions, murder, adultery, fornication, theft, false witness, slander. These are what defile a person, but to eat with unwashed hands does not defile' (Matthew 15:17-20; cf. Mark 7:14-23).

Especially notable here is that for Jesus, and so for Christianity, sexuality is one of God's good gifts; neither for men nor for women is it a cause of impurity. Christians are, however, called to use this gift humanely and responsibly.

6. Christians have a duty to show the proper respect due to God. It is, for example, the custom in the Catholic Church to sign oneself with holy water on entering a church or chapel, or for the priest to wash his hands during the celebration of the Eucharist, as a symbol of purity of heart. The emphasis, however, is on purity of heart, as is made clear by the prayers

of penitence at the beginning of the celebration of the Eucharist.

7. Christians pray for the Church, for political leaders, for all people and also for themselves. They pray for those close to them and for those for whom they are responsible. They should learn to pray frequently and wholeheartedly for their Muslim neighbours, and should also ask their Muslim friends to pray for them; Christians and Muslims would thus express the relationship before God in which they stand together.

8. As regards shared prayer between Christians and Muslims, there are various possibilities:

(a) Public church services. There should be no objection to Muslims coming to churches and other places of prayer for a visit and a time of silent prayer, or even, if they wish, to attend official services of Christian prayer as silent guests. However, active and explicit participation in the liturgical prayers of the Church, such as the monastic cycle of prayer or the Eucharist, assumes membership in the Church as a believing community; such participation in liturgical prayer is in itself a confession of committed belief in the Christian faith. It is a quite different matter respectfully to invite Muslims to take part in our prayers as silent guests, in the spirit of the fellowship created by faith in the One God. Muslims will naturally understand the need to respect the dignity of the place and its local customs.

(b) When a public Christian church service concerns a Muslim directly – as for example in the case of a funeral, an interreligious wedding or a baptism in the family of Christian relatives, neighbours or friends – they will understand that such ceremonies have a distinctively Christian character. This applies equally to rituals and texts. At the same time, however, the Church's liturgical guidelines regarding the selection of readings and the sermon provide for some adaptation in view of the different participants and the relevant circumstances. Significant modifications of the rituals can be considered, especially when a particular ritual might be offensive to adherents of other religions. It is also quite possible to use certain Muslim spiritual texts, preferably unofficial texts, such as the prayers of Muslim mystics. In contrast, the use of Qur'anic or Muslim liturgical texts is usually inadvisable. At funerals, Muslims have occasionally been asked to recite the *Fâtiha*[51] over the deceased person – and they have been grateful for this. It is important, however, to work within the guidelines of the local church and to avoid actions which would endanger good relations between the different communities.

(c) At public interreligious events – such as prayer-meetings, conferences and lectures – each religious group, one after another, might be expected to read a text from its own tradition (from the Bible or Qur'an, for example) with quiet sensitivity to the others present. It should be noted that on such occasions Muslims are normally unwilling to say the first two words of the 'Our Father', and also that the *Fâtiha* (the opening sura of the Qur'an), whose words have biblical roots throughout, is generally regarded as an official prayer, normally reserved for Muslims.

(d) Greater flexibility is possible for small groups of Muslims and Christians who know each other well and are conscious of the danger of syncretism. Here it is possible to say together unofficial texts of the kind mentioned above in paragraph (b), possibly from the mystics of both traditions, or indeed texts written by members of the group itself. Spontaneous prayer is also possible here. Basic prayers of both faiths, such as the 'Our Father' or the *Fâtiha*, can be recited together, provided that everybody present has agreed to this and that nobody present feels spiritually pressurized.[52] Much will depend on the atmosphere of the group in question.

(e) If a group of Muslims, children or adults, ask for a prayer room within a Christian institution, for example in a Christian school, this request should be granted. There is a range of opinions in Europe on whether it is prudent and appropriate for churches and chapels no longer used by Christians to be made available, either for rent or to be purchased, to be used for Islamic worship or for other activities of the Muslim community.

Chapter 9

Religion and the World

I. Muslim Questions

▸ Christianity is one-sided in its preoccupation with spiritual matters; it is exclusively concerned with the salvation of people's souls in the hereafter. But what does it have to say about life in this world – especially about social and political matters?

▸ The separation of state and religion is alien to Islam; it is a Western and Christian idea.

▸ Christianity distinguishes between the things that are God's and the things that are Caesar's. How then should one understand ventures carried out in the name of Christianity such as the crusades and colonialism?

II. Muslim Perspectives

General

Islam understands itself as the final revealed religion, fulfilling and superseding all earlier religions. Judaism is one-sided in its preoccupation with this world; Christianity is one-sided in its emphasis on the spiritual. Islam, in contrast, is the perfect, harmonious religion of the middle way (cf. Qur'an 5:3 and the reference to *dîn wasat* at 2:143, which is interpreted in this sense of a mediating religion). Islam concerns body *and* soul, social, political and religious life, prosperity in this world and in the hereafter. Christianity, on the other hand, sacrifices

89

the body to the soul; it deals only with religion (*dîn*) and ignores politics and the state (*dawla*), setting no store by prosperity in this world, but rather laying all its hope on heaven.

To varying degrees, such ideas are widespread among Muslims.[53] It should be acknowledged that several features of the image which Christianity offered in the 19th century lent support to this grossly oversimplified view. Typical in this regard are phrases like 'the saving of souls' in 'this valley of tears'; a widespread negative view of the body and especially of sexuality, which at times was portrayed as sin's chief domain; the concepts of Christianity as a private religion and of politics as a 'dirty business', and so on.

Many Muslims regard monasticism and the practice of celibacy for the sake of the faith as a typically Christian phenomenon which leaves its stamp on the whole of Christianity. They see in it an embodiment of a 'flight from the world' (*al-firâr min al-dunyâ*) which the 'healthy' perspective of Islam firmly rejects.

It should, however, be noted that this traditional Muslim perspective on Christianity has in recent years undergone a partial change. Muslims often declare their interest in the efforts of the Christian churches to gain a hearing in the sphere of politics and public opinion for issues of peace and justice in the name of the poor, the marginalized and the oppressed. Muslim thinkers are interested in Liberation Theology because it issues a call to struggle against political oppression and social injustice.

Detailed

The unity of God is the central message of the Qur'an. At the same time, Islam, unambiguously charged by the Qur'an to practise social justice, has, from its earliest days in Mecca, taken the side of the poor, the orphans and the powerless, and has struggled against their oppression by the rich. From the beginning, the message of the Resurrection and of the Last Judgement proclaimed by Muhammad aimed to warn the rich of the punishment awaiting them if they did not amend their lives.

This proclamation, which stretches through the whole Meccan period, attacked a social order dominated by the interests of the rich. It led to the persecution of the small Muslim community in Mecca.

Not long after the Hijra to Medina in 622[54] a firmly structured community arose around the Prophet. It grew stronger and soon brought Mecca and the whole of Arabia under its power. The Qur'anic revelation during the 10 years in Medina (622-632) is therefore concerned not only with prescriptions for spiritual life (prayer, fasting, virtues and vices), but also with life in society, covering the organisation of the life of the individual, the family and of society as a whole (contracts, marriage, inheritance); the regulation of political life (instructions for the conduct of war and the division of booty, the duties of leaders, the need for consultation); and, finally, laws on everyday matters, including the regulation of the status of non-Muslims.

The Muslim tradition was naturally shaped by these historical developments and by the emphases in the text of the Qur'ân which accompanied them; from these the tradition developed the theory of Islam as an all-embracing way of life, suited to all human needs: those of the body *and* of the soul; those of the individual *and* of society and of politics. *Al-Islâm dîn wa dawla*: Islam is both religion and state. It is concerned with human beings both in this world (*al-dunyâ*) *and* in the hereafter (*al-âkhira*). 'The good Muslim is not the one who cares so much about this present life that he loses sight of the future; the good Muslim is not the one who sacrifices this life for the one to come; rather, the good Muslim is the one who knows how to use aright both the present and also the future life' (Hadîth).

Islam rejects the separation of the spiritual and the worldly (or the temporal); however, it does recognize the distinction between them. The classical treatises distinguish between acts of worship (*ibâdat*), which are regarded as unchanging, and social relationships (*mu 'âmalât*), which can change. A hadith records the following answer of Muhammad to someone who asked about correct behaviour in the world: 'You are more

91

knowledgeable than I about the things of this world' (*Antum a lamu bi-amri dunyâ-kum*). The commentary of Baidawi[55] on Qur'an 43:63 adds: 'This is the reason why the prophets were not sent to explain worldly matters, but only religious matters.'

In the course of Muhammad's lifetime, i.e., during the period of the Qur'anic revelation itself, a significant development within Islam took place, with the movement from a moral and social vision calling into question existing social structures to the actual establishment of a state religion. In the immediately following period of Islamic history the Caliph (the Prophet's successor) became 'God's shadow on earth' and 'the commander of the faithful' (*amîr al-mu'minîn*). He and his representatives were entrusted with worldly, not primarily spiritual, power, for Islam knows neither a religious hierarchy nor an official teaching office. The Caliphs nevertheless bore religious responsibility for 'commanding the good and forbidding the evil' (*al-amr bi-l-ma rûf wa-l-nahy 'an al-munkar*). According to Louis Massignon (1883-1962), Islam is 'an egalitarian lay theocracy'. Since the creation of modern Muslim states Islam as religion and state (*dîn wa dawla*) thus naturally evolved into the state religion (*dîn al-dawla*), with a few exceptions such as Syria or Yemen. On the other hand, outside the Arab world a number of states with populations including large Muslim majorities are organized on secular principles and appear to wish to remain so (Turkey, Senegal, Mali, Niger, etc).

Since the beginning of the 20th century some Muslim thinkers have become aware of the drawbacks of a state religion. Under this political arrangement religion limits the role of the state, which can easily become the instrument of a religious ideology. Another casualty of this arrangement is religion itself, in a narrower sense, as it is often used as the instrument of the party in power, so that, for example, sermons in the mosques are under the control of government officials. So for some decades in the Islamic world there has been a loud call for a separation of religion and state, and even for a secular state.[56]

These ideas have found an echo in Egypt, Syria, the

Maghreb and Pakistan, not to mention socialist and Marxist thinkers throughout the Muslim world. On the other hand, conservative circles oppose them vigorously.[57] They identify the idea of a secular state as 'a western and Christian heresy', and go so far as to accuse modern Muslim states of disloyalty to the Qur'an. Countless Muslims fluctuate between these two tendencies of complete integration and total separation of religion and state. On the one hand they value the benefits of a state religion, as long as it provides for religious instruction in schools and counteracts the danger of a decay in religious practice. On the other hand, they also see that a religion established by the state scarcely promotes a genuine, personally responsible faith, chosen for its own sake.

III. Christian Perspectives

1. Christian Anthropology

Neither the Old nor the New Testament knows anything of a separation of body and soul, or of a denigration of the body. According to the Bible, the human being is a body endowed with life and spirit. According to older biblical conceptions, the whole being goes down to Sheol, the place of the dead. It took a long time for references to the resurrection to find their way into the Bible (Daniel 12:2-3). The 'resurrection of the righteous' is mentioned first in the latest parts of the Old Testament and above all in the Wisdom books. In the New Testament the Resurrection of Jesus and, in him, of believers, belongs to the core of the message. A bodily resurrection awaits human beings.

The body will participate in the final consummation of all things as a 'spiritual body' (cf. 1 Corinthians 15:44). When Paul says that 'flesh and blood' cannot inherit the kingdom of God (1 Corinthians 15:50) and that believers should not let themselves be governed by the flesh (cf. Romans 8:4-9), this implies no disrespect for the body and the bodily dimension of human life. 'Flesh' (*sarx* in Greek) – as distinct from 'body' (*soma*) – rather signifies human beings in their sinfulness and opposition to God. The point is thus to be led, not by the 'desires of the flesh', but by the Spirit of God (cf. Galatians 5:13-26). By the Spirit of

God the human body is not conquered, but rather made alive (cf. Romans 8:11).

Through the influence of the Greek philosophy of Plato (427-347 B.C.) and of Plotinus (205-270) on Christian thought in the early Christian centuries there developed an emphasis on the human soul in contrast to the human body.[58] Particularly in Gnosticism this led to a fundamental outlook that was hostile to the body, the world and history; this certainly had its consequences in Christianity. The Church, however, differentiated itself from Gnosticism. It is precisely the belief that it is not only the human soul that will be perfected but also the body that will be raised that signals the rejection of a one-sided emphasis on the spiritual. Human beings are created by God as body and soul in unity. The whole human person in all dimensions (including sexuality, for example), is to be liberated from the power of sin and death and led to the freedom and glory of the children of God (cf. Romans 8:21).

2. Religion and State – Faith and Politics

In historical terms, Christianity and Islam have developed in similar ways. Initially, they both proclaimed a spiritual message with social implications, a message which raised questions about unjust political and social structures. In both cases, the very success of the religious message gave them dominating positions in society and led to both Christianity and Islam becoming state religions.

Christianity first became a state religion in the fourth century of its history, under the Emperors Constantine (reigned 306-337) and Theodosius I (reigned 379-395). In the New Testament, however, there is nowhere any basis for the idea of a 'Christian state'. Jesus neither founded a state nor established a Christian society in competition with other political societies. The Christian is a citizen among other citizens, endowed with the same rights and duties as any other citizen, even when the ruling elite of a particular state might happen to be pagans.[59]

The perspective of Jesus and of the New Testament on

this question can be summarized by mentioning two positions which are rejected:

♦ Worldly honour and power are rejected in favour of the kingdom of God. 'My kingdom is not from this world' (John 18:36); 'Give therefore to the emperor the things that are the emperor's, and to God the things that are God's' (Matthew 22:21; cf. 17:27), which implies showing respect to the rights and claims of the worldly ruler, whose authority derives from God. Whenever the crowd wanted to make him king, Jesus withdrew (John 6:15; 12:12-36 [Palm Sunday]). The disappointment of the people over Jesus' rejection of worldly power was one of the reasons for his death, for they expected a triumphant Messiah. A 'triumphalistic' Christianity, which enjoys worldly power and claims this for itself, contradicts the Gospel. Christianity is 'the religion of the cross'; the only success which it seeks – or should seek – is the conversion of hearts to the one Lord.

♦ Christianity rejects all political and social injustice. Jesus' own life consisted of a continuous and often public confrontation with religious and secular power wherever these violated human rights, especially the rights of the poor. This was a further reason for his death. The good news of God's kingdom, which is particularly promised to the poor, must be given priority over the claims of Caesar, i.e., political power in this world.[60] Love of God cannot be separated from love of neighbour; love of one's neighbour is evidence of love of God. In extreme cases this can mean laying down one's life for the sake of one's neighbour (John 15:13; Matthew 25:40; 1 John 3:16; 4:20). Conflicts can lead Christians to the point of self-sacrifice for their brothers and sisters, possibly through resistance to clear injustice. In this sense, political involvement is an essential constituent part of Christian mission.

From the time of Emperors Constantine and Theodosius I onwards Christianity was the state religion for centuries. In some states it has held this status, in a diminished form, up to the present. The weakness or vacuum in the political structures during the final stages of the Roman Empire led the papacy to acquire worldly power; this is the origin of the Papal States. Since practically all its inhabitants were Christians, the theory of the two swords was developed, i.e., the teaching of the spiritual and of the worldly swords, both united in the hands of the Pope, who considered himself to be authorized to appoint kings and emperors. This uniting of both powers in one institution and person led to the Church sanctioning or even initiating and carrying through policies and activities that clearly contradicted the spirit of the Gospel: crusades, imperial and colonial ventures and the Inquisition.[61]

The 2nd Vatican Council turned decisively back towards the spirit of the Gospel.[62] It demanded the independence of the Church (and religion) from political authority, and of political authority from the Church (and religion), while it also called for both to work together to resolve questions separating them from each other. At the same time, it claimed the right for religious communities to exercise influence on society according to standards derived from the values of the Gospel.[63] For the Protestant Church the Barmen Declaration of 1934 was of particular significance.

3. Life in this World and in the Hereafter

The Resurrection of Jesus Christ brings in the end of the ages. Eternal life has already begun: 'I am the resurrection and the life' (John 11:25; cf. 5:24; 1 John 3:14; Romans 6:5). 'This is eternal life, that they may know you, the only true God, and Jesus Christ whom you have sent' (John 17:3; cf. 3:15-16; 5:24; 6:40,47). Eternal life has begun, but it is not yet fully present. The Christian lives in the tension between the 'already' and the 'not yet', because the expectation of salvation in its fullness – through the Resurrection of Jesus and in the Christian faith – has not yet been totally realized. The world must be further transformed by the power of the Holy Spirit, moving towards the closest possible convergence with the will of God.

The perfecting of the creation by God's Spirit will be fulfilled at the return of Christ, which will mark the end of the world and so also of time and history. It is not that a different world will then come into being but rather that this world will be thoroughly renewed and transformed, this same world in which we live, with the same people, but transformed and perfected. This is no mere Utopian hope, for it is founded on Jesus Christ, in his proclamation, his sacrifice of his life and his Resurrection. At the same time, this hope remains realistic; the Christian knows that the transformation of humanity and the world will remain incomplete until the return of Christ.[64]

The Christian faith calls for full involvement in the world, in an attitude of service, in order to contribute to the permeation of the world by the message of the Gospel, so that the world might reach its true destiny. The Gospel also calls for active involvement in pursuit of the welfare of humanity. This can take various forms: working for a political party, which at a particular time and place can be the most suitable way to put into practice the values of the Gospel in collaboration with others, even non-Christians and atheists; or active participation in a trade union; or social service of various kinds. Even the contemplative life is a definite contribution to the fulfilment of human life. However, the Gospel can never be identified with a particular political programme. The task of the Christian thus includes a critical relationship to every political or social system, with the necessary respect for the autonomy of temporal structures and with the necessary attitude of self-criticism directed towards oneself and the Church.[65]

IV. Christian Answers

1. Body and Soul

The unity of the human being should be emphasized. The human person is created by God as a unity of body and soul; it is this whole person, not simply the soul, that is created in the image of God. Consequently reverence and respect are due to the body and also to sexuality.

97

2. Religion and State

The abuse and betrayal of the Gospel in the history of Christianity are to be admitted, although historical context must always be taken into account. At the same time, Christians and Muslims, both separately and together, ought to give critical consideration to their history. There is a need for an intelligent critique of shared Christian-Islamic history, on the part both of Muslims and Christians.[66] We should not only be looking to the past but also to the future, giving our shared support to a political system which encourages religious freedom and mutual respect.[67]

3. This World and the Hereafter

Belief in life beyond death should not lead to indifference and withdrawal from the arena of this world's problems. On the contrary, this belief should motivate efforts to serve our brothers and sisters, especially those who are disadvantaged. It should strengthen our hope and our longing to work for a better world, but at the same time should help us not to identify human projects with the kingdom of God. The end of time will also mean the Last Judgement. Only then will justice be fully realized. At the Last Judgement people will be judged according to their works and particularly according to how they have treated the poor, the marginalized and the oppressed. Here Bible and Qur'an agree. Respect for the rights of God (*huqûq Allâh*) begins with respect for human rights (*huqûq al-insân*). The biblical command to love God includes the command to love one's neighbour and therefore to respect human rights.[68]

Chapter 10

Celibacy as a Religious Vocation

I. Muslim Questions

▶ Why don't priests and members of religious orders marry?

II. Muslim Perspectives

General

1. Islam teaches that it is the natural vocation of every man and woman to establish a family and to take upon themselves, as believers, the associated demands and risks. The establishing and the bringing up of a family are thus considered a duty towards the wider community, both human and religious. Muslims therefore suspect that someone capable of marriage who willingly remains single does so out of selfishness, or alternatively because of impotence or deep disappointment following unhappiness in love. Muslims also doubt whether the obligations involved in the oath of celibacy are really observed: they suspect secret relationships between priests and members of religious orders, as well as homosexual relationships. Underlying all this is the general conviction that healthy men and women cannot live without sexual relations.

2. Furthermore, marriage is a basic duty for believers: 'Marriage is half of the faith' (*al-zawâj nisf al-imân*), in the words of a much-quoted hadith. This is especially so for men, whose duty it is to 'protect the weaker sex'. It is thus understandable why voluntary celibacy is something of a scandal among Muslims and evokes hostile criticism, though this spontaneous and basic reaction appears today to be undergoing certain developments.

3. Cases of voluntary celibacy in the Islamic world, among both men and women, have recently become more frequent. This phenomenon, which can sometimes be on a temporary basis, can arise from the need for dedication to a particular cause, as with older brothers and sisters looking after the younger children in a family, nurses or social workers devoting themselves wholly to their work, or freedom fighters such as the *fidâ'iyyûn* and *fidâ'iyyât* of the Palestinian struggle for liberation. It can also arise from personal reasons, such as the desire to seek fulfilment in life outside or before marriage, or from religious reasons, as with unmarried pilgrims (*hâjjiyyûn*) or young widows who have decided to stay in Mecca to pray and meditate, either for a particular period or for their whole life.

4. Those who know priests and members of religious orders and have experienced their daily lives recognize that the vocation of celibacy can genuinely be lived out. Many admire this way of living. This is often the case with Muslim girls who live or work together with nuns, would like to live as Muslim celibates and express their regret that there is no comparable form of religious life in Islam. What are their motives? The desire to escape from marriage, or the longing for a life of dedication? Muslims will often say: 'That is in order for Christians, but "in Islam there is no monasticism" (la *rahbâniyyat fil-Islâm*).'

Detailed

1. With a few exceptions, one can say that celibacy as a vocation is not recognized in Islam, either as a religious or a

human ideal. There is practically no trace of it in the Qur'an. The Prophet was married. There are many hadith which, while explicitly praising marriage, portray celibacy negatively and reject it. For example: 'Our *sunna* (tradition, and implying upright character) is marriage' (*sunnatu-nâ al-zawâj*); 'Marriage is half of the faith'; 'If I had one day more to live and was not married, I would take a wife, so that I should not meet God as an unmarried man'; it was said to a man who was not yet married: 'So you have decided to live in Satan's community? If you wish to become a Christian monk, then enter their community openly, but if you are one of us then follow our *sunna!*'

One of the greatest Muslim theologians, al-Ghazâli (1058-1111), explains in great detail why marriage is a binding obligation in Islam:

♦ to beget offspring, in obedience to the clear will of God and the Prophet;

♦ to strengthen the Muslim community;

♦ to satisfy one's sensual appetites and to gain a foretaste of Paradise here on earth;

♦ for the husband: the benefit of having someone to look after the housework, so leaving time free for prayer;

♦ for the mystic: relaxation through enjoying oneself with one's wife;

♦ finally, an opportunity to grow in patience through tolerating one's wife's temperament.[69]

Nearly all Islamic mystics were married.

2. However, celibacy is not totally ignored nor rejected in every case. The Qur'an praises Mary as the perfect example of virginal purity: she 'guarded her chastity' (Qur'an 21:91; 66:12; cf. 3:39, referring to John the Baptist [*Yahyâ*], who was chaste [*hasûr*], and hinting at the chastity of Jesus). Monks are praised in the Qur'an (5:82; 24:36-37 and 57:27; but note also 9:31,34). Some Muslim mystics and ascetics lived as celibates, as, for example, the famous female mystic

Râbi 'a of Basra, whose refusal to marry seems to imply an oath of dedication to God. The manuals of some religious orders (e.g., the Rahmâniyya and Bektâshiyya) praise celibacy undertaken for religious motives. In a discussion of 'Arguments for and against Marriage', Al-Ghazâli presents celibacy as advisable only if one is not ready for the expenses and burdens of a family, if the character of the proposed wife is too difficult or if she would prevent the mystic from engaging in the serious practice of meditation. He comes to the conclusion that the value of being or not being married depends on one's circumstances. The ideal is to be able to combine married life with piety and devotion to God, as the Prophet Muhammad did.

On the celibacy of Jesus, al-Ghazâli comments:

> Perhaps he was so disposed by nature that being preoccupied with family matters would have exhausted him too much, or it would have become too difficult for him to provide for a family lawfully, or he was unable to combine marriage with devotion to the service of God and chose devotion to the service of God alone.[70]

III. Christian Perspectives

It is not a question here of singleness in a secular context, which is not concerned with sexual abstinence. It is a question of the conscious Christian motivation for celibacy, particularly the celibacy and sexual abstinence demanded of priests and members of religious orders.

1. Catholic Perspective

For the Catholic faith there are three fundamental and complementary motives for the vocation to celibacy:

♦ for the sake of the kingdom of heaven (Matthew 19:12) or (with Paul) for the sake of the proclamation of the Gospel (1 Corinthians 9). It is a matter of showing one's total gratitude to and love for Jesus Christ. For those who are called to celibacy, this way of life can deepen inner union with God and increase openness for God. Celibacy can be an expression of expectancy before God and the awaiting of his kingdom;

♦ the service of others, which is furthered by total devotion to this calling;

♦ a conscious imitation of Jesus, who lived as a celibate, and of Mary, who is called 'the Virgin' in the Creed. This has inspired and motivated very many Christians who are celibate for the sake of Jesus.

2. Protestant Perspective

Marriage is recommended as being of equal status to celibacy, for which there is no particular preference. Celibacy can be significant for the sake of dedicated service in the proclamation of the Gospel, but it is not demanded of ministers. Celibacy is lived out in some communities, but not on the basis of an irreversible commitment. The celibacy of Jesus is not seen as having any vital function, though Jesus does serve as an example to those who are celibate. The same does not apply to Mary; biblical scholars assume that Mary did not at all live as a permanent virgin, but rather had further children after Jesus (Mark 6:3).

IV. (Catholic) Christian Perspectives

1. In response to the Muslim suspicion of selfishness as a motive, one can answer that vocation to celibacy is, in principle, motivated by the desire to serve others (*li-khidmat al-insâniyya*) and by the will to do good (*li-l-a mâl al-khayriyya*). This, however, demands of celibates that they are truly available for the service of others. It will not carry much conviction if their way of life is scarcely any different from that of married people. Celibacy can truly be lived out as a Christian vocation only when the whole way of life is pervaded by the spirit of the Gospel.

2. Where emphasis is laid on the religious and moral duty to marry and bring up a family, one can in response point to

the fact that celibacy aims at total dedication to God (*li-wajh Allâh; aslama wajha-hu li-llâh*), and is undertaken for the sake of prayer. This assumes that the spirit of total devotion and prayer can actually be noticed.

3. Where there is the suspicion that disappointment in love lies behind the decision to become celibate, one can point to the value and the beauty of married life, of the Christian family as an ideal, and, possibly, to happily married sisters and brothers.

4. One should neither conceal nor deny the struggles and temptations involved in celibacy, nor give the impression that it is a protection against all crises. One must recognize that many have left this way, finding that it was too difficult for them.

5. When questioned on this subject, priests and other members of religious orders ought to explain how they experienced their vocation as a call, an invitation (*da 'wà*) from God to grow in love, and also a desire to follow the example of Jesus and of the Virgin Mary. One can describe how this call matured through prayer, reflection and consultation with other believing Christians, with the support of one's family, if this was the case; and of how the idea finally became so clear and pressing that to reject it would have brought about much sadness and distress. This all assumes that in the life of a person genuinely living out the religious vocation to celibacy authentic human and spiritual fulfilment becomes palpable.

Chapter II

Religious Pluralism and Freedom of Religion

I. Muslim Questions

▶ Why are there so many religions if God has endowed all people with the same human nature?

▶ Every religion, Christianity above all, claims to be universal. How can different religions be 'universal'? Only one can really be universal. The other religions can thus only be considered as partially or provisionally true.

▶ Must one not rather assume the idea of a universal religion, a kind of synthesis of all religions?

▶ These days the Church speaks about religious freedom, but it was not always so. In the past, the Church made use of imperialism and colonialism for its own ends. If it has now become an advocate of religious freedom isn't this just because it can no longer get its own way?

▶ Religious freedom is good in principle, but can people be allowed to turn their backs on the true religion and convert to another religion? Doesn't the principle of religious freedom constitute a danger, threatening the religions themselves?

▶ How can someone read the Qur'an and not become a Muslim? Such a person must be a hypocrite, like the orientalists.

II. Muslim Perspectives

General

1. Islam is the one true, perfect and enduring religion. It has absorbed into itself everything of any worth in the other religions. The Muslim who thinks in traditional terms is therefore astonished that there are still Jews and Christians today, for with the advent of Islam these religions essentially became irrelevant. Judaism and Christianity are of a provisional nature and at best only partially true. They were intended for limited human communities. Outside Islam religion is of no genuine value because Islam is the only religion that is truly universal.

2. 'Wars of religion' are a historical reality. In the past, they took place between the Islamic and the Christian worlds, between Catholics and Protestants. Even today there are still conflicts in the name of religion, in, for example, Lebanon, Northern Ireland, the Philippines, Sudan, etc.

3. Many Muslims assume as a certain fact the collaboration between Christianity and imperialism, colonialism and nationalism.

4. There cannot be a right to change religion. A person is born as a member of a given religion and must stay within it as it constitutes an essential element of personal, collective and national identity. Conversion to Islam is of course an exception, because here it is a case of entering a society and a structure which replace all other identities and make them unnecessary.

Detailed

1. The whole Qur'an is pervaded by a longing for all people to be united in one single religious community, the *Umma*, as was God's will from the beginning. However, people soon divided themselves into different religions, each one claiming to be the one true religion (10:19; 11:118; 21:92; 43:33).

2. Islam is the final religion and is perfect, exclusive and universal. It was proclaimed by Muhammad, the 'Seal of the Prophets', as the only true way to attain salvation (3:19,73,85,110; 5:3; 9:33; 43:28; 61:9). 'It is he who has sent his messenger with guidance and the religion of truth, to proclaim it over all religion, even though the pagans may detest it' (9:33; cf. 61:9). It is consequently only logical that Islam and its claims apply to the whole of humanity (7:158; 34:28). Other religions are either false (as with idolatry or polytheism) or provisional and only partially true (as with the 'religions of the book', Judaism and Christianity). This unique religion must spread everywhere, through proclamation (da 'wà, 'calling' or 'inviting' to Islam, equivalent to the Christian concept of 'mission') and, if necessary, through the sword. From a historical perspective, Islam started with peaceful exhortation and steadfastness in the face of persecution (in Mecca); later it also took up the sword (in Medina). After the Prophet's death the 'great conquests' 'opened' the way for Islam into many countries. In the following centuries Muslims fought numerous wars, both in aggression and in self-defence, in the name of Islam. In general, the conversion of populations to Islam took place gradually and peacefully, both in areas already conquered by Islam and also outside the world controlled by Islam. In this process an outstanding role was played by Muslim traders and by the religious brotherhoods. The effect of social pressure on non-Muslims should also not be underestimated, however, especially in the context of Muslim-majority societies. Contemporary Muslim apologists emphasize that Islam was proclaimed in an exclusively peaceful manner, but they fail to mention the wars fought under the banner of Islam (fî sabîl Allâh, literally 'in the way of God'). According to the apologists, such wars, if it is conceded that they happened at all, were always fought in self-defence.

3. The Qur'an proclaims the principle that everyone is free either to believe or not to believe (10:40-45; 17:84,89,107), together with the other principle so often repeated today:

'No compulsion in religion' (*lâ ikrâha fîl-dîn*, 2:256). But the Qur'an also says clearly that polytheists must believe or be put to death (9:5; 48:16). On the other hand, the 'People of the Book' (Jews and Christians) are offered the status of protected people (*dhimma*): they may maintain their religion – even though it is faulty and has been superseded by Islam – along with its hierarchy and its rituals, but they must pay a special tax (*jizya*) and remain 'small' (i.e. inconspicuous and subordinate) (9:29). The Muslim who abandons his religion, either through conversion to another religion or by deeds or words clearly directed against Islam, will be condemned by God (3:85-90; 4:137; 16:108) and must be punished with death (2:217 has consistently been interpreted thus by legal scholars, and this interpretation has been reinforced by numerous hadith).

4. In recent times many Islamic countries, through their representatives on the United Nations Commission on Human Rights, have declared their agreement with the principle of religious freedom, as it is formulated in the Universal Declaration of Human Rights (Article 18, emphasizing freedom of thought, conscience and religion), but with the restriction that nobody is permitted to turn away from the true religion (i.e., Islam).[71]

5. Influenced by the contemporary cultural context and ideological pluralism, many Muslims have developed the attitude, widespread in the West today, which holds that all people should be allowed to follow their conscience. Other Muslims say that all religions are of equal value and, furthermore, that Islam and Christianity are very closely related, if not quite identical in terms of content. Although such statements are made, they are generally not to be understood as reflecting syncretism or indifference in religious matters. Rather, they testify to an attitude of brotherliness among those who wish to live on the basis of faith. Some Muslims support the idea of a universal religion, even if in practice this would amount to a form of syncretism. Finally, there are Muslims who believe that the

religions – and in the first place Christianity and Islam – should enter into a genuine dialogue, trying to come closer together as brothers and letting God lead us together as far as he will. The overarching aim should be to present a shared witness in our world to faith in God.

III. Christian Perspectives

1. The good news, as proclaimed and lived out by Jesus, consists of the revelation of God as the Father of all people, as all-encompassing, unconditional love, with a particular love for the humiliated, the poor, the sinners, the marginalized and oppressed. It is the will of Jesus that he wishes to gather together his own people and all peoples in this love of God. All people – and in the first place the 'poor' – are called into the 'kingdom of God', that is, into the dominion of the love of God.

2. In the New Testament, which testifies to the faith of the earliest apostolic Church, Jesus Christ, the Word of God, is the highest, final and definitive revelation of God. In Jesus Christ God turns to all people; Christianity is thus in its very essence universal. History shows that from its earliest days onwards the Church has understood its mission to be universal, knowing itself to be a servant of the universal love of God, who reconciles all things to himself (cf. 2 Corinthians 5:18-21; Ephesians 2:11-12).

3. From a historical perspective, Christianity arose and was spread on the basis of the dynamic faith of the apostles and of the first Christian generations. Their witness and proclamation were effective despite, or even because of, persecution. After the Edict of Milan (313 A.D.), which guaranteed full religious freedom to the Church, thus leading to the Church soon becoming the official religion of the Empire, Christianity became entangled in various violent conflicts, sharing in responsibility for the persecution of heretics and bringing social pressure to bear on them. These conflicts were essentially political in nature, but were presented as Christian causes in order to gain as much

support for them as possible. The Crusades were a quite different case, for here religious motivation (the liberation of the Holy Sepulchre) was clearly the primary motive. The relationship between colonialism and mission should not be understood in terms of one uniform pattern. In some cases missionaries accompanied or followed the colonialists (e.g., the Portuguese and Spanish in the 15th and 16th centuries); in other cases the missionaries arrived first (in Central Africa, China and Japan); in yet other cases missionaries opposed colonialism (e.g., Las Casas in Latin America; French West Africa).

4. The evaluation of non-Christian religions from the perspective of the Christian faith has undergone a long process of development: from Justin (d. 165), who spoke of spiritual seeds waiting in all people for the Word of God in order to bear fruit; to the position of Augustine of Hippo (354-430), who, deploying rhetoric which we might find oversubtle, considered even the virtues of the pagans as vices; and on to the theories which concede to unbelievers good faith (*bona fides*) and hold that they will not be condemned. More recently, some theologians have taught that there are elements in the faith and in the moral values of the nations and cultures of the world which await their fulfilment and clarification in the light of the Incarnation of God in Jesus Christ. This leads into the predominant views today.

Among the recent attempts to develop an adequate theology of the non-Christian religions, two deserve particular attention; the second of these has had the wider impact.

(a) Emphasis on the distinction between faith and religion: this theory was chiefly expounded by the Protestant theologians Karl Barth (1886-1968) and Dietrich Bonhoeffer (1906-1945), and later, with modifications, taken over by Catholic thinkers such as Jean Daniélou (1905-1974). Religion is understood here as a natural movement of the human creature towards God. The religions are the collective manifestation of religion, translating it into rituals, forms of piety, etc. In the view of at least the early Barth the religions are seen as mere human products and are set negatively over against faith in the revealed Word. Daniélou evaluates them more positively: every human group, every civilization, has its own religion, so that one can speak of Celtic, Germanic, Mediterranean, African and Indian religion, and also in the Christian religion one can find characteristics shared with these religions.

On the other hand, faith is the human response to God's Word, to God, who takes the initiative to encounter his creation and to question it. If religion is the movement of the human soul towards God, then faith is the answer that human beings give to the Word of God that reaches them through revelation. For Daniélou, faith in Jesus Christ must 'incarnate' itself in each religion. Since faith is bound up in a contextually relevant manner with the religions and the cultures formed by them, it transforms these and bestows new meaning on their rituals, laws and traditions. Daniélou's conclusion is that by accepting the Christian faith human beings 'do not move from one religion to another', but rather that their own religion is reshaped and transformed.

(b) Distinction between general and special revelation: this new approach was chiefly developed by Karl Rahner (1904-1984) and then, in its essential aspects, taken over by several other authors. Since the beginning of human life on earth, God has never ceased to communicate with all people. This 'general' revelation is attested to in the Bible, in the stories of Adam and Noah, the Book of Wisdom and Paul's Letter to the Romans (1:19ff.). The great non-Christian religions are the higher manifestations of this general revelation. But then the word of God appeared in a 'special' way in the history of the people of God, beginning with Abraham, through the patriarchs and prophets, and finally, 'in these last days', through Jesus Christ, the Word of God become flesh and the fullness of revelation. In this 'special' revelation God's self-communication, which also takes place in 'general' revelation, can be contemplated in history, so to speak; it has a human face: Jesus of Nazareth. 'Whoever has seen me has seen the Father' (John 14:9). In the light of this revelation the presence of God in all religions is illuminated.

But even the revelation of God in Jesus Christ will only be unveiled in its full significance at the Parousia, or the coming of Christ, at the end of time. Christian proclamation and the dialogue of the Church with the other religions look towards this goal. During the intervening period the history of religions, including the existence of the non-Christian religions, contributes to the 'unveiling of the meaning of revelation'. If understood in this way, the acknowledgement of Jesus Christ as the fullness of revelation, as the revelation of God in a human person, does not at all necessitate that the other religions should be disparaged or that it should be denied that they have some relation to God and that they offer true worship. Rather, it should be understood as an invitation to acknowledge the other revelations as varied contributions to the unveiling of the full meaning of revelation. Christians can thus be enriched in dialogue with the religions.

5. Christianity can only be faithful to the Gospel if it is understood as a message of peace and reconciliation. Jesus clearly and decisively refused to be the political Messiah for whom his own people were waiting. He decided to die rather than engage in political revolution; to forgive, rather than to seek power and to retaliate. Later, as a result of the support given to it by the Emperor Constantine the Great (reigned 306-337), the Church entered into so close a relationship with the state that it at times called for wars, blessed them and justified them. Over recent decades, however, the Church and the popes have endeavoured to use all possible

opportunities to promote peace and justice. Certainly the Church recognizes the right to self-defence, both of individuals and of nations, and also the right, on occasions even the duty, to oppose political regimes which are clearly unjust. However, whenever and wherever possible, Christians should prefer nonviolent action (which is very far from being ineffective) and should make their contribution to the overcoming of the narrowness of theocratic, nationalistic and fanatical religious ideologies with their potential for violence.

6. Faith is a free gift from God, to be freely received or rejected by people. History, however, knows of 'conversions' which came about through compulsion or duress (e.g., Charlemagne's coercion of the Saxons) or of cases where conversions came about because of purely human motives and social factors, or were at least strongly influenced by them.

For a long time the predominant view in the Church was that the best system of church-state relations was that in which Christianity is declared the state religion and in which, therefore, 'error has no rights'. It is true that from its beginnings the Church always demanded the freedom for everyone to be able to accept the Christian faith without being disadvantaged thereby; the Church was of course much more reserved about recognizing the freedom of a Christian to interpret the Christian faith independently, or to give the faith up, or to change over to another religion (cf. the Inquisition). If we are aware of the long and painful development of the idea of religious freedom within Christianity, this can help us achieve a better understanding of certain attitudes, reactions and difficulties on the Muslim side.

Since the 2nd Vatican Council and its Declaration on Religious Freedom, however, the attitude of the Church to this question has been unmistakeably clear, at least at the official level: religious freedom is one of the basic and absolute rights of human beings as such. The way in which mission is carried out must be marked by respect for the worth and the outlook of the other. Mission should be a matter of witness in and through dialogical relationships. Of its very essence, faith can only be presented as an invitation (cf. 2 Corinthians 5:20); faith is always to be proposed not imposed. Every single person remains free and responsible to choose for himself or herself, in the light of conscience and before God.

IV. Christian Answers

1. Religious Pluralism

Religious pluralism is a mystery. It has something to do, on the one hand, with God's respect for human freedom, and, on the other hand, with the natural conditions of human religious and cultural development. For thousands of years the main human groups lived in isolation from each other, in Europe, in Asia and in America. Today, in contrast, the world is characterized by a diversity of interconnections and by a consciousness of mutual dependence. Of course there are still today various tensions and violent conflicts between human groups. The religions have an important role to play here; they share in responsibility for the achievement of greater justice and harmony in relations between the nations, the economic blocs and the cultural groupings of our world. All conflict between religions – such as polemics and insensitive proselytism – should be avoided, as should syncretism, which destroys the originality and authenticity of religion. Only dialogue, along with the process of mutual learning which it involves, can open the religions up to each other so that people can learn to live together in diversity and get to know and understand each other better. This is not a matter of denying differences but rather of grasping what these differences really amount to. Neither does dialogue in any way exclude witnessing at times to one's own faith and inviting others to recognize what one has oneself come to know as true and valuable. Believers of different religions should try to identify those issues on which a shared, believing witness is possible, together with a genuine search for unity, in humble submission to God's will.

2. The Plurality of 'Universal' Religions

It is a fact that Islam and Christianity both claim to be universally valid. There is no reason why either should give up this claim. Everything depends on the methods used as the two religions seek to express and live out their universal claims. Today there should be no place for methods which rest chiefly on individual or collective ambition: support from political authorities; violence; war; coercion in all its forms and manifestations, whether subtle or otherwise. The only way that is acceptable and worthy before both God and humanity to obtain universal recognition for the values which one holds to be true and valid is through the witness of a living faith and through frank dialogue, along with the necessary respect for the free decision of the human conscience.

3. Religions and Responsibility for War

It must be admitted that in the past religions have been responsible for wars, or have at least shared in responsibility for them, and that we cannot say that this is no longer the case today. The wider picture contains both light and shadows. On more than one occasion in the course of history the religious factor has prevented or moderated violence. One thinks, for example, of 'the truce of God' during the Christian Middle Ages, or of the strict conditions which Islamic Law attached to a 'just war'; or of the care for prisoners of war and innocent victims called for by the religions. Furthermore, the main reason for the so-called wars of religion was not so much hostility between the religions themselves, but much more the pursuit of power on the part of individuals and of human groups (empires, dynasties and nations), in the course of which religion was used in the service of personal or collective ambition. Finally, as regards contemporary conflicts, it is important to examine information critically before alleging simple religious motivation: it would, for example, be simplistic to designate as merely 'religious' the conflicts in Lebanon, Northern Ireland, the Balkans, the Philippines and Afghanistan. The reality is that in most of these cases the religious authorities, far from having incited these conflicts, have on the contrary always been passionately committed to peace and reconciliation.

4. Religious Freedom[72]

Religious freedom is one of the inalienable rights of every human person. To suppress it, or even just to limit it, is to mock both God and humanity. It is the union between religion and the state (or, even today, the union between nationalism and the state or between practical atheism of a capitalist or socialist kind with the state apparatus) which has been primarily responsible for significant abuses in this area, both in the past and still today. All religions have the right to liberate themselves from such systems and totally to overcome the resistance of these systems to the effective implementation of religious freedom.

All people, whether Christian or Muslim, are committed to living in solidarity with their own religious community or group and to seeking its peace and prosperity, whether this is the *Umma*, the Church or other groups. At the same time it is important to show full respect for free decisions made in good conscience in regard to faith and religious adherence. The one binding principle in this sphere is to follow the voice of one's own conscience, that is, the conscience which is genuinely seeking the truth. The testing and setting right of hearts is a matter for God alone. Faith and religion can only be genuine if people are totally free to choose or to reject them. We are thus all challenged to continue to seek God's will.

Chapter 12

The Heart of Christianity

I. Muslim Questions

In some cases a Muslim who does not have defined, specific questions about this or that Christian doctrine may nevertheless ask – out of curiosity or personal interest – 'What is the essence of Christianity? What is its chief characteristic? What is at its heart?' This chapter therefore sets out to demonstrate how first Muslims and then also Christians understand what is at the heart of Christianity.

II. Muslim Perspectives

General

1. Generally speaking, Muslims are deeply convinced that Islam is the last, most perfect and most comprehensive of all revealed religions. Other religions, Judaism and Christianity above all, were valid before Islam but have now been superseded. The true religion is Islam, and only Muslims can be saved.

   At the same time, Muslims can be quite open towards certain religious values which they meet in the lives of Christians. This, however, only increases their astonishment that people who have encountered Islam, and have even studied it, remain Christians rather than gratefully taking

117

the opportunity to find the fulfilment of all their expectations in Islam, the true and final religion. Muslims might think that it is perhaps an emotional attachment to 'Western' religion and culture, an attachment that cannot be rationally justified, that prevents Christians from being open to Islam. Or are there other motives?

2. Other Muslims offer more detailed arguments. The religion of Jesus, it is argued, is Islam, i.e., the message of the one God and the call to serve him alone. However, Christians distorted this message very early on, and Paul, in particular, is denounced for this distortion. For others, the principal fault lies with the union of the Church with the power of the state since the days of Constantine the Great. Whatever is the case, the original Gospel of Jesus has been 'corrupted'.[73]

3. Other Muslims again take the view that the perspective on the historical Jesus derived from the work of some biblical scholars is also significant for Muslims, as this perspective calls into question the historical basis of some of the Christian beliefs about Jesus which Muslims do not share. Muslims therefore reject the central doctrines of the Christian faith as misinterpretations of the true message of Jesus. The result of this misinterpretation or 'corruption' (tahrif), Muslims argue, is the existence of four Gospels (rather than the original one Gospel) in the New Testament available today.

4. An interesting, if also thoroughly subjective, perspective was offered by Kamil Hussein, an Egyptian medical doctor, man of letters and religious thinker[74]. In his view, the essence of the message of Moses was the fear of God; of Jesus, love; and of Muhammad, the hope of Paradise. He accordingly explains the meaning of Christianity as follows: 'To believe, deep in one's soul, that what calls us to do good is the love of God, which also calls us to love everyone whom God loves; and also to avoid everything that harms other people, because God loves all people without distinction; and, finally, to know that we cannot love God if we harm his friends, that is, other people'.[75]

5. One can therefore encounter today among Muslims two contrasting assessments of Christianity:

   (a) Positive. Christianity is a 'religion of the book', originating from Abraham along with Judaism and Islam. It is a revealed ('heavenly') religion. Christians are thus close to Muslims; they are not hostile to them (Qur'an 5:82). They are believers, and all believers are brothers (49:10). They are monotheists. They pray. They feel responsible for the general welfare of humanity; Christianity demands of its adherents that they show love for the poor.

   (b) Negative. Christians are unbelievers (*kuffar*) and polytheists (*mushrikun*). They worship a human being, Jesus, and make him into a god. They believe in three gods (Mary and Jesus alongside Allah). Their faith is very complicated, while Islam is straightforward. Their Scripture, the Gospel, has been 'altered' and 'corrupted' and no longer exists in its original form. Their religion has been superseded by Islam. The Church and its teaching office have suppressed freedom of thought and condemned science (e.g., the case of Galileo Galilei, 1564-1642). Christians reject Islam and its belief in the radical oneness of God and in Muhammad as the last of the prophets. When they pray they do not follow rules; they do not fast. Their religion is onesidedly spiritual and makes unnatural demands such as celibacy; it despises the body and is obsessed with the idea and the omnipresence of sin.

Detail

1. The Qur'an presents two positions which diverge from each other: one praises Christianity while the other is hostile to it. Both tendencies are to be found in Islam, taken as a whole, both in the past and also today.

   (a) The positive tendency. We encounter this above all in the unreserved admiration shown for the religious figures who are particularly dear to Christians: Jesus, his mother

Mary, the apostles, John the Baptist, Zechariah and so on. This admiration also extends to the Gospel as a book, which was sent down upon Jesus and is acknowledged by the Qur'an, although of course only in its original text and its authentic, 'uncorrupted' meaning. According to the witness of the Qur'an there were also, at the time of the Prophet, Christians close to Islam, described as 'the nearest in love' (5:82) and 'bowing in humility to Allah' (3:199; cf. 3:110,113,115; 4:55; 5:66). The Qur'anic perspective on monks and priests, however, appears to be thoroughly ambivalent (5:82; 24:36-37; 57:27, on the one hand; 9:31,34, on the other).

(b) The negative tendency. This is chiefly concerned with Christian doctrine about God and Jesus. Christians have made Jesus into a god and they call him the Son of God (4:71; 5:17,72; 43:59; 9:30-31); they worship three gods and allege that Jesus was crucified (4:156; cf. 3:55). Furthermore, they take 'their monks to be their lords in derogation of Allah' (9:31). They commit excesses in their religion (4:171) and have separated into sects on the basis of their different views on the person of Jesus (5:14; 19:37; cf. 2:133,145; 3:61). They claim that only Christians can enter Paradise (2:111). They call themselves God's children and his beloved friends, but God will punish them for their transgressions. The Jews and Christians ('the People of the Book') 'wish they could turn you back to infidelity after you have believed, from selfish envy, after the truth has become manifest to them' (2:109; cf. 3:110); and the monks (as well as the Jewish rabbis) 'devour men's wealth' (9:34).

This contradictory perspective doubtless reflects the conflicting attitudes of Christians to Muhammad and the Qur'an: some accepted them while others opposed them. This conflict is reflected in the Qur'an, so that Christians are at one point reckoned as a privileged group, 'the People of the Book', and at another point as an accursed group of unbelievers (*kuffar*) and of polytheistic idolaters (*mushrikun*). It is precisely this ambivalence that has determined the character of Muslim attitudes to Christianity right up to the present. The ways in which Christianity and Christians are judged – whether as unbelievers or as 'People of the Book' and monotheists – thus depend to a considerable extent on the peaceful or tense co-existence of Christians and Muslims, exactly as in the time of the Prophet.

2. The same two-sided perspective is present in Islamic tradition and theology, although they tend to emphasize the negative statements in the Qur'an. We must keep in mind this twofold inheritance: on the one hand the traditional condemnation of Christian doctrines and moral teachings, often in association with Western neo-colonialism and an allegedly corrupt Western civilization; on the other hand the quite different perspective, also rooted in the Qur'an, which regards Christianity as one of the three monotheistic (or 'heavenly') religions, and Christians as brothers and sisters in genuine faith in God (Qur'an 49:10, as long as Christians are included among the 'believers' mentioned here).

Within the negative perspective, three aspects are particularly to be noted:

(a) Christianity overstates the nature of the relationship between the Creator and the creation by speaking of a mutual love between God the 'Father' and human beings as 'his children';

(b) its emphasis on the spiritual dimension is also overstated, so that its exclusive interest in the life to come and in the soul are at the expense of this life and the body, just as also the individual is emphasized while the significance of the social dimension of life is neglected – all this in contrast to Islam, the religion that addresses human beings in their entirety;

(c) finally, Christianity does not sufficiently respect the transcendence of God, because it considers Jesus to be both human and God at the same time and so also speaks of 'the participation of human beings in the divine life'.

III. Christian Perspectives

Among many other dimensions of Christianity which might have been chosen, two are emphasized in what follows.

1. Christianity as the Way of Love

i.   The term 'Christian' was first applied to followers of Jesus by Gentiles in Antioch (present-day Antakya in South-eastern Turkey) around 43 A.D. (cf. Acts 11:26). To be a Christian means to believe that Jesus, the prophet from Nazareth, who 'went about doing good' (Acts 10:38) and who died on the cross and rose from the dead, is the Christ (the Messiah), the one who came forth from God as God's final and definitive self-revelation to human beings. Following the example of Jesus, and in his power, Christians try to live out their relationship to God and other people in harmony with God's will and in the service of others. The will of God is that we should love all people – who are all called to become God's children – with the same love; we are called to love both God and our brothers and sisters.

Christians believe that Jesus, who died on the cross, was raised from the dead and now shares in the glory of God the Father, is living and present always and everywhere.

ii. During his life on earth, Jesus revealed that God is Father: his own Father, the Father of Christians and the Father of all people (cf. John 5:18; 20:17; Matthew 6:9 and parallels). It is the will of this Father-God that all people should understand themselves as his children. By expressing the relationship between God and the human race in terms of 'father' and 'son', Jesus chooses a powerful image to express God's love: the love of a father for his children.[76] For the Christian, however, this does not imply fatherhood in a physical sense on the part of God towards his creation.[77]

Jesus brings alive in his own distinctive way an essential feature of the understanding of God in the Old Testament (the Torah): God loves his people with a passionate love, as a mother loves her children (Isaiah 49:14-15; cf. Hosea 11:1-4); as a husband loves his wife, even when she is unfaithful (Hosea 1-3; Ezekiel 16); as a man loves his fiancée (Song of Songs). Jesus reveals the fullness of God's unconditional love for the human race. This went much further than was imaginable in the time of Jesus, when God's love was thought to extend only to the Jews and indeed only to the righteous among the Jewish people. This understanding excluded from the 'kingdom of God' not only non-Jews, but also Jews who were considered to be open sinners (such as tax officials), and also those who suffered from contagious illnesses such as leprosy.

Jesus turned this understanding of the relationship between God and human beings totally on its head. He proclaimed that God turns to all people with the same love. God, the Father of all people, loves them all without distinction. If it is at all possible to speak of God having a 'special' love for anyone, it would be for those whom society condemns and excludes: open sinners (who repent) and Gentiles: 'The tax collectors and the prostitutes are going into the kingdom of God ahead of you' (Matthew 21:31; cf. 8:10; Luke 7:36-50).

This explains why Jesus, acting in accordance with the revelation of God as the universal and merciful Father, was always ready to welcome those, such as the poor and notorious sinners, who turned to him to find a way out of their material or spiritual need. Jesus never rejected anyone, accepting invitations equally from people of high standing and Pharisees as well as from tax collectors and sinners. Was he not criticized for sharing meals with sinners (Matthew 8:10; 11:19; 21:31; 9:10-13; Luke 7:36-50; 15:1-2,7,10; 19:7)? Precisely in this sense, he said that he had 'come to call not the righteous but sinners' (Matthew 9:13; Mark 2:17; Luke 5:32). He was severe with those who were proud of their 'righteousness' and at the same time condemned 'sinners', the poor and Gentiles (Matthew 23:3,13-36; Luke 11:42-52; 18:9-14), for, he taught, 'there will be more joy in heaven over one sinner who repents than over ninety-nine righteous persons who need no repentance' (Luke 15:7,10). This divine attitude to sinners is presented wonderfully in the parable of the prodigal son (Luke 15:11-32) and in other parables with God's compassion as their main theme (Luke 13-15). Jesus struggled against everything that divided human beings into the two camps of the virtuous and the sinners. He himself relativized some of the most sacrosanct regulations in the Jewish Law, for example concerning the Sabbath (Matthew 12:8; Mark 2:27; John 5:6) or the restriction of worship to the temple in Jerusalem (John 2:13-17; 4:20-21). For 'the Sabbath was made for humankind, and not humankind for the Sabbath' (Mark 2:27). If the leaders of the Jewish people condemned Jesus to death and pressed for him to be executed by the Romans, this was because he had proclaimed God's unconditional readiness to forgive and be reconciled. This message put in question the very basis of the authority of the leaders of the people. God the Father appeared to be of one mind with these leaders, since he gave a free hand to those who took Jesus to the cross. However, God did not abandon him to the power of death (cf. Acts 2:27), but raised him from the dead, 'the firstborn of the dead' (Colossians 1:18; Acts 26:23; Revelation 1:5) and seated him at his right hand. 'And of that all of us are witnesses', said Peter (Acts 2:32). So Jesus is truly Lord, endowed with the very authority of God, the God who solemnly confirmed the message of Jesus, the truth of all that he had said about God and about humanity.

iii. This message is the message of boundless love, the love of God who loves all people and invites them all to become his children; the God who 'makes his sun rise on the evil and the good, and sends rain on the righteous and the unrighteous' (Matthew 5:45).

iv. It is thus natural that Jesus declares the commandment to love to be the most important commandment in the Law.

124

'You shall love the Lord your God with all your heart, and with all your soul, and with all your mind. . . You shall love your neighbour as yourself' (Matthew 22:37,39). Love for God and love for other people were already linked in the Old Testament (Deuteronomy 6:5; Leviticus 19:18) and Jesus takes this up. He makes it into the 'new law' (John 13:34), not only because for him it serves as the summary of 'all the Law and the prophets' (Matthew 22:40; 7:12; Luke 6:31), but because through Jesus a new significance will be given to this love for God and neighbour.

The love of God, the Father of all people, demands love for all people, all of whom God truly loves as his own children. For Jews in the time of Jesus, the fellow Jew was the neighbour who was to be loved. For Jesus, however, every person is to be loved, including sinners and even one's enemies; indeed it gradually became clear to him and to the early Christians that even the Gentiles and the adherents of other religions (such as Samaritans, Syro-Phoenicians and Romans) were included in this commandment. The disciples of Jesus were challenged so to love one another that, in Jesus' words, 'everyone will know that you are my disciples' (John 13:35; 15:12-17). Love extends to enemies and persecutors:

> You have heard that it was said: "You shall love your neighbour and hate your enemy." But I say to you, Love your enemies and pray for those who persecute you, so that you may be children of your Father in heaven; for he makes his sun rise on the evil and on the good, and sends rain on the righteous and on the unrighteous. For if you love those who love you, what reward do you have? Do not even the tax collectors do the same? And if you greet only your brothers and sisters, what more are you doing than others? Do not even the Gentiles do the same? Be perfect, therefore, as your heavenly Father is perfect (Matthew 5:43-48).

Instead of returning evil for evil, they should return good for evil (Matthew 5:38-42); they should forgive without measure or limit (Matthew 18:21-22), exactly as God forgives (Matthew 6:12, in the 'Our Father'), and as Jesus forgave those who nailed him to the cross (Luke 23:34). This does not imply being indifferent to what is evil and unjust or even applauding it, but rather forgiving wicked and unjust people, because only forgiveness can liberate people from evil and bring about their reconciliation with God and with each other.

This love knows no boundaries, because it is indeed an image of the love of God, who forgives, reconciles and creates peace, and because it consists in the gift of itself to others, to God as well as to neighbours. Love does not seek its own advantage. It consists in the giving away of itself and so also in for-giving: 'No one has greater love than this, to lay down one's life for one's friends' (John 15:13). Finally, Jesus was not content simply to preach about such love; he lived it, and he sacrificed his own life for all people, even for his enemies, whom he forgave on the cross.

Only after the death and Resurrection of Jesus did the apostles and the early Christians fully understand that the core of the life and the teaching of Jesus consisted in love, in God's love for us and our love for God and unlimited love for all people. They went so far as to say that the real test of love for God is love for one's neighbour (1 John; especially 4:20-21), love that consists 'not in word or speech, but in truth and action' (1 John 3:18). 'We know love by this, that he laid down his life for us – and we ought to lay down our lives for one another' (1 John 3:16). And in fact the early Christians did live out this close community of brotherly love (Acts 2:42-46; 20:7-11). Reflecting on the life and message of Jesus in the light which they received from the Holy Spirit, the apostles finally began to understand: if it was possible for Jesus, in the way that has been described, to reveal so clearly the essence of God's love and also to live out the perfect response to this love, then this was ultimately possible only because he was 'God's Son' in a very particular and unique way, sent by the Father to communicate this quality of love. For God is love (1 John 4:8-16) and his love 'was revealed among us in this way: God sent his only Son into the world so that we might live through him' (1 John 4:9). This loving God 'became flesh and lived among us, and we have seen his glory' (John 1:14). Jesus, the Word of God, is the revelation of God's love because he is his Son. Of course, this revelation of love in and through Jesus must be received by the whole human race and furthermore translated into action, till the end of time, through the power of God, the Holy Spirit, working both in the Church and beyond it.

Paul's emphasis is that only the Spirit of God, sent by Jesus after his Resurrection (John 7:37-38; 16:7-15), can make it possible for us to call God our Father (Romans 8:15; Galatians 4:6) and to love him and other people with the same love which we have received from God (1 Thessalonians 4:9; Romans 5:5; 15:30; cf. 1 John 4:7). In his 'hymn to love', Paul holds that every one of our actions receives its value from love, and that without love even the most precious charisms are worthless.

v.   The official Christian doctrines, or dogmas, that emerged in the early Christian centuries reflected the significance of Jesus Christ as this was elaborated in arguments with the chief religious and philosophical currents of that time. They sought to defend the faith of the New Testament in a changed context.

vi. Christianity therefore means following the way of love, whose source is God himself (1 John 4:7) and who is revealed to us in Jesus, the Son of the Father, in his preaching and also in his life, death and Resurrection. The Church of Christ is based on this love; this love is the source of its life.

The exercise of authority in the Church is in the first place a form of service of the community of the disciples of Jesus, following the model of the love which lives in God's very self. The exercise of this authority consequently demands love

127

for Jesus that is prepared to show itself in costly service (cf. Jesus' dialogue with Peter at John 21:15-17: 'Do you love me?. . . Feed my sheep'). However, this community of love among Christians should of course never become narcissistic, directed only inwards. It is essentially witness, 'so that the world may believe' (John 17:21). It is a duty for every single Christian, as well as for the Christian community as a whole, to be witnesses to love in the world, committed to justice, reconciliation and peace. This is a high ideal, scarcely ever fully realized in practice, but one towards which all Christians must continually aspire, according to the measure of the gifts they have received. In the course of history, unfortunately, Christians in general and the Church in particular have repeatedly failed to be faithful to this ideal; this sad and regrettable reality must be recognized honestly.[78] Nevertheless, the good news of Jesus continues to be present and active, today as yesterday. It presses the Church to live by the law of this love and to work for it to be more widely spread in the world, tearing down every barrier – racial, social or religious – that divides human beings, struggling against the root sins of selfishness and hatred. Every Christian is called by Christ to be unconditionally committed to the victory of love.

Excursus: Islam and the Love of God

To maintain that love for God and for neighbour is the central and essential commandment of Christianity does not mean that other religions, and Islam in particular, are simply unaware of this twofold commandment, or that it is only truly Christians who are concerned about love and live lives empowered by love. There is in fact a way of love in Islam, practised by many Muslims, normally without reference to the teaching of Jesus or Christianity.

i. There are only a few verses in the Qur'an which speak explicitly of the love of God, whether the love of God for human beings (God as *al-wadud* – 'full of loving-kindness' [11:90; 85:14]; God who 'casts' his love [*mahabba*] on Moses

[20:39]) or the love of human beings for God (four references at 2:165; 3:31; 5:54). There are also two verses which speak of mutual love between God and 'a people whom he loves and who love him'; at 5:54 this is in the context of *jihad*, here understood as physical struggle against the unbelievers, a 'holy war'. However, on the basis of these Qur'anic verses we cannot say that the love of God for human beings and of human beings for God is a central theme of Islam. The one and only God, the just and merciful judge, is the centre of the Qur'anic message. Love is, however, a theme in the Qur'an and Hadith and also in the teaching of classical Islam, providing both content and terminology for the spiritual tradition within Islam to draw upon.

ii. This spiritual tradition is principally that of the Muslim mystics, the Sufis. Starting with the remarkable Rabi'a in the 8th century A.D., the Sufis made love for God (rather than the love of God for human beings) into the central axis of their search for God. The great Sufis of the early Islamic centuries absorbed this 'way of love' into orthodox Islam, thanks principally to Muhammad al-Ghazali (d. 1111), who emphasized that only God is worthy to be loved and who regarded this love (*mahabba*) as the highpoint and goal of his spiritual quest. Later the ideal of love for God was spread through the whole Muslim world by the religious brotherhoods. It became an important theme for meditation and was entirely accepted by official Islam.

This love of human beings for God, as distinct from the love of God for human beings, bears typically Islamic characteristics. For love is seen as a longing for something that is lacking, and the God of Islamic faith is quite free of such dependence. In Muslim understanding, love is a longing for God, a longing to come nearer to him; any idea of loving union between God and human beings is, however, strictly excluded. Finally, this love for God can also demand love for our neighbour, but it is not at all the case that love for created beings can or should be placed

129

on the same level with love for the Creator. Many Muslim mystics, including Rabi' a and al-Ghazali, were of the view that to dedicate oneself totally to God it is necessary to distance oneself as far as possible from all created things.

2. Christianity as the Way to Human Fulfilment

i. For believers, Christian or Muslim, human beings are the creation of 'God's hand', formed after his likeness and destined to return to him. This is the fundamental calling of the individual, of the human race, and indeed of the whole creation, which longs for liberation from every form of oppression, in order finally to enter into God's glory (Romans 8:19-25; Qur'an 81; 82; 99; 101). This shared calling establishes a basic likeness between all people, transcending differences of race, social standing and religion.

ii. The position held by the Qur'an within the structure of the Islamic faith corresponds to that held in Christianity by the person of Jesus himself, the Word of God. Christianity thus offers primarily not teaching but a way, the way of discipleship of Jesus. Every person is called to become God's adoptive son or daughter in Jesus Christ (Ephesians 1:5). Between the Creator and his creation reciprocal love holds sway. The Creator is Father; human beings are his children. The intimacy of this relationship is far greater than that between servant (*'abd*) and Lord (*rabb*). The Christian is called to love God and all people because all people are brothers and sisters of Jesus and children of the same Father.

Loving God and other people is the only real way to attain human fulfilment. This goes far beyond the natural love between people, for Jesus demands that we should not return evil for evil but rather persist in forgiving and even loving our enemies. Nobody is capable of such love in his or her own strength. Rather, it is a gift from God, whose gift consists in enabling us to love our brothers and sisters as he himself loves them. Jesus himself lived this message out to the point of dying on the cross. To reject faith in this

God – whatever the personal explanations for such a rejection might be – is to deprive human beings of their ultimate meaning.

iii. The kingdom of God remains a goal not yet attained, a destination not yet reached. Human fulfilment in this world will never be perfectly realized. Hope for total fulfilment is the great energy that drives the human race forward. Progress, in every sense, always remains a possibility till the end of time and, on the individual level, till death. For many, death is seen as proof of the vanity and meaninglessness of human life, but for the believer the death of Jesus on the cross opens the way to his Resurrection and that of all people. Jesus transforms death into victory over death. The end of human life and the end of the world on the last day open the way to 'eternal life', to its final fulfilment. Then every person will see God face to face in the new heaven and the new earth. There humanity and the whole creation will discover their final and perfect consummation (Romans 8:22-23).

iv. The value of human beings rests on the fact that they have been created in the image of God (Genesis 1:26-27, quoted in 1 Corinthians 11:7; Colossians 3:10; James 3:9) and in the image of Christ (John 1:3; Romans 8:29; 1 Corinthians 8:6; Colossians 1:16; Hebrews 1:2). The human person should therefore never become a means to an end. His or her rights must be respected by every kind of authority, whether secular, religious, social or political.

But the human person can only find fulfilment within a community of free and independent persons. The family and other forms of human community therefore play indispensable roles at both national and international levels. The rights of the individual and of communities must therefore be balanced in carefully weighted relationships. Human communities, secular and religious, serve the common good to the extent that they value the individual person.

Excursus: Muslim Humanism[79]

Christianity is not the only religion that claims to offer a comprehensive vision of humanity, its origins and its destiny. Islam makes a similar claim. Muslim and Christian humanism have much in common. However, insofar as Christian humanism has its centre in Christ and Muslim humanism in the Qur'an, there are essential differences of emphasis.

The Qur'an teaches that God created Adam with his hands (38:75), forming him from clay (7:12; cf. 23:12; 32:7); the creation of human beings from the male's sperm is also often mentioned (22:5; 32:8; 80:19). God also breathed his 'spirit' into Adam (15:29; 32:9; 38:72). A famous hadith teaches, in terms very similar to Genesis 1:26, that human beings have been created in the image of God.

The human race was created to worship the one God, to serve him, to obey him, to praise him and to thank him (4:1; 51:56; 3:190-191; 7:172; 30:17-18). Man is a mortal creature (*bashar*) and is often rebellious. Nevertheless, he is charged with bearing witness to the one God (7:172-173).

Those who reject faith in the one God are to be compared to animals (25:44; 8:55; 22:18). Human beings have a higher status. Only to Adam did God reveal the names of all the animals – something which even the angels did not know (2:31-33). God therefore commanded the angels to prostrate themselves before Adam immediately after his creation. Only Satan (*Iblis*) refused to do this (15:31; 18:50; 19:44; 20:116; 38:74). The human race is to rule the created world, which God has made subservient to man's command and his use (14:32-33; 16:12-14; 22:65). Man is God's 'vicegerent on earth' (2:30), a phrase often cited by modern authors advocating a Muslim humanism.[80]

Notes

1 Translations of passages from the Qur'an are based on the widely available translation by 'Abdullah Yusuf 'Ali, frequently reprinted since it was first published in 1934. All otherwise unattributed references of the type '2:2', '5:82', '112' should be understood to refer to the Qur'an, the first number referring to the Qur'anic *sura* (chapter), and the number after the colon to the *aya* (verse).

2 On the Gospel of Barnabas see note 73 below.

3 Biblical quotations are from the *New Revised Standard Version*.

4 Ibn Sînâ (980-1037), Ibn Khaldûn (1332-1406), Muhammad 'Abduh (1849-1905), Sayyid Ahmad Khan (1817-1898).

5 'Abbâs Mahmûd al-'Aqqâd (1889-1964), author of the life of Jesus *'Abqariyyat al-Masîh* (1952) - see Olaf H. Schumann, *Der Christus der Muslime*, Böhlau: Cologne/Vienna, 1988, pp.111-131; Fathî Uthmân (b. 1928 in Upper Egypt), author of *Ma'a al-Masîh fi anâjîl al-arba'a* (With Christ in the four Gospels) (1961) – see Olaf H. Schumann, op. cit., pp.132-146; Khâlid Muhammad Khâlid (b. 1920), author of *Ma'an, 'ala al-tarîq, Muhammad wa-l-Masîh* (Together on the way – Muhammad and Christ, 1958) – see *The Oxford Encyclopaedia of the Modern Islamic World*, II, pp. 412-413.

6 Mohamed Arkoun (b. 1928, Algeria), Professor of the History of Islamic Thought and Culture at the Sorbonne, Paris; Nasr Abu Zaid (b. 1943, Egypt), Professor of Islamic Studies at Leiden.

7 Norman P. Tanner (ed.), *Decrees of the Ecumenical Councils*, vol. 1, London/Washington, 1990, p. 232.

8 *Geist und Leben*, 46 (1973) pp. 81-85; p. 82 for this quotation.

9 2nd Vatican Council, *Declaration on the Relationship of the Church to Non-Christian Religions: Nostra Aetate*, 4. Quotations from the documents of the 2nd Vatican Council in this volume are from *The documents of Vatican II*, eds Walter M. Abbott and Joseph Gallagher, Geoffrey Chapman, London/Dublin, 1966.

10 Islam's central sanctuary: a large cubic building, now situated at the middle of the great mosque at Mecca.

11 The term 'Hijra' refers to the migration of the Prophet Muhammad in September 622 from Mecca to Yathrib (later known as Medina, i.e., 'the city [of the Prophet]').

12 See the following comments of Werner H. Schmidt and Gerhard Delling on prophecy in *Wörterbuch zur Bibel*, Furche, Hamburg, 1971, p. 442: 'The prophet speaks from the future; he does not start from the present in order to proceed into an unknown future, but rather takes coming events as his starting point. He does not seek

to proclaim the Law, to apportion blame, or to criticize prevailing circumstances, but rather to announce judgement or promise salvation; the present must be seen in the light of what is to come. Awareness of the future brings insight into present reality and how events are developing – not the other way round.'

13   For Justin on 'seeds of the Word' (*logoi spermatikoi*), see his 2nd Apology 8.1.

14   GRIC, *Ces Ecritures qui nous questionnent: la Bible et le Coran*, Le Centurion, Paris, 1987 (English translation: *The Challenge of the Scriptures: the Bible and the Qur'an*, Orbis, New York, 1989).

15   Kenneth Cragg, *Muhammad and the Christian: a Question of Response*, Darton, Longman and Todd, London and Orbis, New York, 1987.

16   *Dogmatic Constitution on the Church: Lumen Gentium*, 16; *Nostra Aetate*, 3.

17   These observations are relevant where dialogue takes place between Christians and Muslims who wish to remain faithful to their respective beliefs. Naturally Christians have the duty – as indeed do Muslims, on the basis of the Qur'an – to proclaim their faith. How exactly this should happen and what are the proper means to do so, however, is a problem beyond the scope of the present work.

18   *Nostra Aetate*, 3.

19   *How to Understand Islam*, SCM Press, London, 1989, pp. 140-148.

20   See in particular the following chapters of this study: 'The Divinity of Jesus and the Incarnation'; 'Cross, Sin, Redemption'; 'God, the Three in One'.

21   There is evidence in the Qur'an of the influence of contemporary Christian groups which thought in terms of a Trinity of God the Father, God the Mother and God the Son. 'In the *Arabic Infancy Gospel* Mary is repeatedly referred to as "exalted, divine Mary".' See Martin Bauschke, *Jesus – Stein des Anstoßes*, Böhlau, Cologne, 2000, p. 155.

22   Second Vatican Council, *Dogmatic Constitution on Divine Revelation: Dei Verbum*, 4.

23   *Nostra Aetate*, 1.

24   The concepts 'nature', 'substance' and particularly 'person' originate from the philosophy of that time, when their meanings were different from what they are today. The doctrinal content of these concepts can only be correctly preserved by identifying the metaphysical significance which they had at the time of the Councils. Thus 'person' (translating *hypostasis*) indicates that God acts and lives in relationships. However, if one understands 'person' in the sense of an individual personality, an autonomous centre of psychological

consciousness, then one is making the Councils mean precisely the opposite of what they intended. 'Person' would then indicate what the Councils sought to express by the concept 'nature', and it would thus follow that there are three distinct 'natures' in God.

25   If one wishes to use Arabic terminology, the Trinity should be referred to not by the noun *tathlîth*, but rather by the adjective *thalûth*. *Tathlîth* conveys the inappropriate idea of the division of an object into three parts.

26   With regard to the dialogue over Jesus as the Son of God, one does well, bearing sura 112 in mind, to use the concept *ibn Allâh* and never *walad Allâh*. To convey a metaphorical sense, Arabic only ever uses *ibn*, e.g., *ibn al-sabîl*. In this context, a passage from the famous Muslim scholar al-Biruni (973-c. 1050) is of interest: 'Passing from the word *God* to those of *father* and *son*, we must state that Islam is not liberal in the use of them; for in Arabic the word *son* [ibn] means nearly always as much as a *child* [*walad*] in the natural order of things, and from the ideas involved in parentage and birth can never be derived any expression meaning the Eternal Lord of creation. Other languages, however, take much more liberty in this respect; so that if people address a man by *father*, it is nearly the same as if they addressed him by *sir*. As is well known, phrases of this kind have become so prevalent among the Christians, that anybody who does not always use the words *father* and *son* in addressing people would scarcely be considered as one of them. By the *son* they understand most especially Jesus, but apply it also to others besides him. It is Jesus who orders his disciples to say in prayer, "O our *father* which art in heaven (St. Mt 6,9)", and informing them of his approaching death, he says that he is going to his *father* and to their *father* (St John 20,17). In most of his speeches he explains the word the *son* as meaning himself, that he is the *son* of *man*' (Al-Biruni, *Ta'rîkh al-Hind*, Ed. Sachau, London, 1919, chapter 3; here we have reproduced the English translation by E. Sachau, *Alberuni's India*, English text. Vol. 1, p. 38.).

27   This explanation should be clearly distinguished from the so-called Modalism of the 3rd century. The Modalists were 'monarchian' in their understanding of God, saying that there is only one God, the Father, with whom Jesus, as Christ, is identical. Consequently they said that it is the Father who became human, suffered and died on the cross (Patripassianism); the Son and the Spirit are only different 'names'. This doctrine, which occurred in various different shades and colours, developed into Sabellianism, named after Sabellius, who lived at the end of the 3rd century. Finally, in the 4th century, it took the form of Arianism, which asserted that the Son is no more than a created being. This all developed as a reaction against trinitarianism and reflected the monotheism originating in the

Hellenistic philosophy of the Stoics and the Neo-Platonists. It was the Council of Nicaea (325) which condemned these heresies with the affirmation that the Son is at one and the same time truly God, 'consubstantial' with the Father, and truly human.

28   Wahhabis are followers of the teaching of Muhammad Ibn Abd al-Wahhâb (1703-1793), who strove vehemently against every form of mediation between the Creator and the creation, such as the cult of saints, Shi'ite concepts of the imam and monistic tendencies in philosophy and mysticism.

29   Unless otherwise indicated, 'Catholic' will here mean 'Roman Catholic' and 'Protestant' will refer to the Lutheran and Reformed traditions of Germany.

30   During the first Christian decades it was chiefly adults who were admitted to the Church through baptism. The New Testament does not provide conclusive proof of the baptism of children, but neither does it exclude it. The practice of baptising the children of Christian parents at a very young age is justified on the grounds that the parents undertake to bring children up in the faith, so that at a later stage they might consciously confess the faith for themselves and commit themselves as adults to the Church. Some churches baptize only adults and maintain that the baptism of children contradicts the Gospel.

31   Confessio Augustana, article 7.

32   *Lumen Gentium*, 21 (*in communione hierarchica*); cf. also *Lumen Gentium*, 8 and 10.

33   The Arabic-Muslim terms *ma 'sûm* and *'isma* are often rendered as 'infallible' and 'infallibility'. However, they express rather more the idea of being protected; their more exact meaning is 'protection from sin'. This can apply to the prophets, or, for the Shi'ites, to the successors of 'Ali whom they know as 'imams'. The concept is thus normally understood in the sense of 'freedom from sin', rather than in the sense of 'infallibility'.

34   *Lumen Gentium*, 12

35   *Lumen Gentium*, 25, referring to the 1st Vatican Council.

36   *Lumen Gentium*, 12.

37   Before being sent to a parish, a priest undergoes spiritual and theological formation in a seminary. After his ordination by the bishop, which takes place in a special festive liturgy, he is sent by the bishop to a particular congregation. There is no fundamental objection to priests being married. In the Middle East there are many married priests and most Orthodox priests are married with children. In the West, in the Latin Church, it has been a canonical regulation since the 7th century that priests should remain unmarried. But this regulation could be changed because priests are not

members of religious orders. Priests should not be equated with members of religious orders, even though many members of religious orders are also priests. Members of religious orders, whether men or women, are Christians with the vocation to dedicate their lives to God in a particular way. Their consecrated life finds concrete expression in the three vows of poverty, chastity (celibacy) and obedience. Members of religious orders live in communities (such as convents) under the authority of a superior. Some orders dedicate themselves above all to prayer (contemplation). Others are chiefly occupied with spiritual teaching and/or the education of young people, others again with medical or general social welfare, and so on. Where their activities are related to the life of a diocese, members of religious orders come under the authority of the bishop. Among Protestants also, church workers are theologically trained, with ministers and theologians undergoing college courses. In most cases, ordination accompanies their sending out to work with congregations or for other church duties. Other church workers are, for example, deacons, church musicians, youth workers and social workers.

38   In the 4th century the Council of Nicaea (325) condemned Arius and the Arians, who considered the Son of God to have been created by the Father. Arian ideas are found today among the Unitarians, who reject the doctrine of the Trinity. In the 5th century the Council of Ephesus (431) condemned Nestorius and the Nestorians, who claimed that there are two persons in Christ. Some 'Nestorian' groups, known as 'Assyrians', have survived in Iraq and Iran. However, in the course of history most of them entered the Catholic Church and are known as 'Chaldaeans'. Also in the 5th century the Council of Chalcedon (451) condemned Eutyches and the Monophysites, who recognized only the divine nature in Christ. Monophysitism is maintained by the Coptic Church in Egypt and its sister church in Ethiopia, as well as the Jacobites in Syria (the 'Syrians') and the Armenians. The Syrian and Egyptian Christians who rejected Monophysitism, accepted the Council of Chalcedon's definition of faith and remained loyal to the Emperor in Constantinople became known as 'Melkites' (derived from the Syriac i.e. 'the Emperor's people'). Today this term is applied to Christians of the Byzantine rite who belong to the Patriarchates of Antioch, Jerusalem and Alexandria, whether Orthodox or 'Uniate' (i.e. united with Rome). In the 11th century a great schism took place between the Eastern Church, under the authority of the Patriarch of Constantinople, and the Western Church, led by the Pope in Rome. Thereafter the Eastern Church designated itself as 'Orthodox' (holding true doctrine) and the Roman Church as 'Catholic' (universal).

The churches of the Reformation arose in the 16th century. Through the work of Martin Luther (1483-1546) the Lutheran churches arose, while the Calvinist or Reformed churches go back to John Calvin (1509-1564). In England the Church separated from Rome during the reign of Henry VIII in the 1530's, with the distinctive Anglican tradition developing over the rest of the 16th century.

39 It should further be noted that in each of the Eastern churches a group of believers ('Uniates') has become reunited with the Catholic Church. There are consequently Orthodox and Catholic Melkites and Orthodox and Catholic Syrians. The same applies to the Copts, the Assyrians and the Armenians. In contrast, the Maronites are all Catholic.

40 Some of the Muslim questions listed in section I above have already been addressed in the course of section III.

41 Legends about the 'wealth' and the 'power' of the Vatican are regularly repeated, with reference, for example, to the 'artistic treasures' in the Vatican Museum. Much of this relates to the political power of the papacy in earlier times. The money necessary today for the administration of the Vatican and to help the worldwide Church is raised almost exclusively from the contribution of believers all round the world.

42 In the Protestant churches infallibility has traditionally been ascribed to the word of God. Synods and other church bodies might wish their decisions to be binding but they can always be revised.

43 On *ijmâ'* and the question of infallibility in the *Umma*, see the discussion above in section II of chapter 6.

44 According to a tradition (hadith), circumcision is obligatory for boys and beneficial for girls; according to another tradition, the circumcision of the clitoris should only be partial. Even today, female circumcision is said to be in accordance with the Shari'a by some Muslim legal scholars: cf. the following hadith: Ibn Hanbal 19794; Abu Dawud 4587; Ibn Maja 600; al-Tirmidhi 101. Female circumcision is practised by Muslims, and also by non-Muslims, particularly in Africa, chiefly because it is believed to encourage large families. On the other hand female circumcision is rejected today in non-Muslim and to some extent also in Muslim circles, including on the grounds that female circumcision can have seriously damaging emotional consequences. In conditions of low hygiene, performing female circumcisions carries a high health risk. Even in Germany, where it is a criminal offence, female circumcision still presents a continuing problem.

45 The principle *ecclesia semper reformanda* (the Church must constantly be reformed), which was freshly emphasized in the 2nd Vatican Council *Decree on Ecumenism: Unitatis Redintegratio* , 6,

has been a basic feature of the Church from the beginning onwards and was an essential source for the Reformation, which led to the formation of the Protestant churches.

46 In everyday usage the meanings of the Arabic term *hulûl* can include: 'descending'; 'stopping'; 'staying'; 'overtaking'; 'arrival'. In Islamic mysticism it indicates the indwelling light in the human soul. It is also used by Christian Arabic authors to translate 'Incarnation', God's becoming human in Christ, though the Arabic text of the Christian Creed uses the term *tajassud*, literally 'taking bodily form', 'materialization'.

47 On this story see above in section II of this chapter.

48 The text of the *Fatiha* (sura 1) is as follows: In the name of Allah, most gracious, most merciful. Praise be to Allah, the Lord of the worlds, Most gracious, most merciful,
Master of the day of Judgement.
You alone do we worship and to you alone do we pray for help.
Guide us in the straight path,
The path of those on whom you have bestowed your grace, not of those against whom you are wrathful, nor of those who go astray.

49 The painting of icons has its origins in Byzantine art, from where it entered into the life of the Orthodox Church. Icon (from the Greek *eikon*) means picture or image. Justification for icons in biblical terms was found in texts such as Colossians 1:15: 'He (Christ) is the image of the invisible God, the firstborn of all creation.' Icons are representations of Christ and the saints. They are symbols of the mystery of Christ. One might say that the painters, who were mainly monks, were writing the Gospel in colours; they saw what they were doing as a holy calling. A collection of icons is presented on the iconostasis, the screen separating the sanctuary from the rest of the church in Orthodox churches.

50 In Catholic belief, the saints are men or women of faith who lived in exemplary ways in their particular situations in life and are therefore an encouragement to believers in their various situations. So, for example, the mother of Jesus, grieving for her son, bearing her pain, is a source of consolation for women in the midst of life's troubles. Catholics are thus accustomed to entrusting their problems and troubles to saints, asking for their prayers. Saints are also intimate companions in life; with their protection one feels safe at home or with the family, for example, or in traffic, on a journey, in sickness and finally at the time of death. St Joseph, for example, is understood to be the patron saint who helps one to achieve a good death. Protestant Christians do not pray to the saints; they do, however, make use of their written prayers.

51 See footnote 48 above.

52 If the *Fâtiha* is recited together, this must be on the assumption that the reference in verse 7 to those who 'go astray' from the 'straight path' is not taken to apply to Jews and Christians.

53 In the 20ᵗʰ century such ideas are expressed in the apologetic writings of the significant reformers Muhammad 'Abduh (Egyptian, d. 1905), Rashid Rida (Syrian, d. 1935) and the Algerian *'alim* Ibn Badis (d. 1940).

54 See above in chapter 4, section II.

55 Al-Baidâwi (d. c. 1290) is a famous, much-quoted commentator on the Qur'an. His commentary is to a large extent a revision and summary of the celebrated commentary on the Qur'an by al-Zamakhshari (d. 1144).

56 The most famous advocate of such reform was the al-Azhar shaikh 'Ali 'Abdurrâziq, author of the 1925 publication *Al-Islâm wa usûl al-hukm* ('Islam and the Sources of Power' [French translation by L. Bercher in *Revue des Études Islamiques*, 1933/III and 1934/II. The text of this translation together with a thorough assessment by the Moroccan scholar Abdou Filali Ansari can be found in 'Ali 'Abdurraziq, *L'Islam et les Fondements du Pouvoir*, ed. Abdou Filali Ansari, Éditions Découverte, Paris, 1994]). 'Abdurraziq argues that the message of the Qur'an is essentially religious and that the organisation of a Muslim state can in no way have been part of Muhammad's task as a prophet. 'Abdurrâziq was condemned by his colleagues, in whose opinion the Medinan period, with its emphasis on the social and political side of the revealed message, represented the intrinsic development and completion of the prophetic task and career. Muslim thinkers who support the separation of state and religion must therefore interpret the Qur'an in a way which, at the most basic level anyway, does not agree with the way in which Muslim tradition has consistently articulated the Medinan period of the Prophet's career. 'Ali 'Abdurrâziq's supporters, in contrast, seek to convince their co-religionists that the traditional interpretation is in error.

57 Especially noteworthy here are the Muslim Brotherhood of Hasan al-Banna (1906-1949) and the Jama'at-i Islami of A. A. Mawdudi (1903-1979).

58 Plato's view was that the human being is essentially a soul, confined in the body, from which it tries to liberate itself in order to find its way to God, free from all hindrance. The Platonic conception of the human being has had a far-reaching influence on Christian thought, up to our own time. Under the influence of modern anthropology, there is a strong tendency today to return to the biblical conception of humanity.

59 With reference to the duties of Christians towards pagan rulers, see Romans 13:1-7; 1 Timothy 2:1-2; Titus 3:1; 1 Peter 2:13-15.

60 'We must obey God rather than any human authority,' say Peter and the apostles (Acts 5:29; cf. 4:19; Matthew 10:18).

61 Until recently, the ideal situation for Christians, according to statements in official documents, was to live in Christian states, even when the popes, beginning with Leo XIII (towards the end of the 19th century) proclaimed the division of Church and state (against the idea of the theocratic state), while reminding the state of its duty to protect the rights of God and of his Church. Cf. the 1885 Encyclical of Leo XIII, *Immortale Dei* and the 2nd Vatican Council *Dogmatic Constitution on the Church: Lumen Gentium*, 38.

62 This was especially clear in the *Declaration on Religious Freedom: Dignitatis Humanae*, 12, where it is acknowledged that 'In the life of the People of God... there have at times appeared ways of acting which were less in accord with the spirit of the Gospel [than the teaching of Christ and of the Apostles] and even opposed to it.'

63 Cf. *Dignitatis Humanae*, 4; the *Pastoral Constitution on the Church in the Modern World: Gaudium et Spes*, 76 and the *Decree on the Bishops' Pastoral Office in the Church: Christus Dominus*, 19-20.

64 The Marxist Utopia, in contrast, claims to be able to bring to effect in the course of history the complete reconciliation of opposing forces.

65 Cf. *Gaudium et Spes*, 43, a text which emphasizes both the relevance of the Gospel to all political programmes, and its transcending of them.

66 Christianity has reached the point of submitting its revealed sources to a new, critical examination; modern Islamic thought is more and more confronted by the same challenge. This comes about particularly through the impact of humanistic and secular movements which emphasize the autonomy of secular structures, and on the basis of historical experience which has shown how significant amalgamation with politics can lead to religion losing its true spirit. This is leading some thinkers in a number of Islamic countries to support the independence of Islam over against the state, and of the state over against Islam. See note 56.

67 The documents of the 2nd Vatican Council, especially *Dignitatis Humanae* and *Gaudium et Spes*, along with the Encyclical *Populorum Progressio* are helpful in this context.

68 The 2nd Vatican Council invites Christians and Muslims 'to make common cause of safeguarding and fostering social justice, moral values, peace, and freedom' (*Nostra Aetate*, 3).

69 See Hans Bauer, *Islamische Ethik. Nach den Originalquellen übersetzt und erläutert.* Volume II. *Von der Ehe.* Max Niemeyer, Halle, 1917, see esp. pp. 3-48; also photographically reprinted, Olms

Verlag, Hildesheim, 1979. (This is a translation of the 12th book of al-Ghazali's major work *Ihyâ Ulûm al-Dîn* [*The Revival of the Religious Sciences*].)

70   Ibid., p. 48

71   See *Islamochristiana* [Rome] 9, 1983, pp. 158-159.

72   With the 2nd Vatican Council's *Declaration on Human Freedom: Dignitatis Humanae*, the Catholic Church committed itself irreversibly to the principle of religious freedom in society.

73   Many Muslims are convinced that the original Gospel revealed to Jesus, as it was before it was 'corrupted', has come to light again recently thanks to the 'discovery' of the 'Gospel of Barnabas'. In reality this is a forgery from the 16th century, produced either by an Andalusian Muslim who had been forcibly converted to Christianity, or by a Muslim living in Venice. Cf. Christine Schirrmacher, *Der Islam*, Volume 2, Hänssler, Neuhausen/Stuttgart, 1994, pp. 268-289; Jan Slomp, 'The Gospel in Dispute,' *Islamochristiana* [Rome] 4, 1978, pp. 67-111; and, for a brief discussion, Kate Zebiri, *Muslims and Christians Face to Face*, Oneworld, Oxford, 1997, pp 45-46.

74   *Al-Wâdi al-Muqaddas* (The Holy Valley), Dar al-Ma'arif, Cairo, 1968. English translation: *The Hallowed Valley. A Muslim Philosophy of Religion*. Cairo, 1977.

75   Ibid., p. 31 of the English translation.

76   The Qur'an also speaks of the love of God in words with powerfully emotional resonances: *mahabba, mawadda, rahma*.

77   See the discussion of this point in section IV of chapter 2 and section IV of chapter 5.

78   See the discussion in section IV of chapter 6.

79   In English, the term 'humanism' is sometimes associated with the rejection of religious belief; here, however, it denotes ways in which, within specifically religious frames of reference, both Muslims and Christians understand the nature, dignity and destiny of the human race.

80   In a profound meditation on Qur'an 33:72, the famous contemporary thinker Muhammad Talbi (b. Tunis, 1921) expounds how God offered the *amâna* (possession of the faith as a trust, or, alternatively, responsibility for governing the world) to the heavens, the earth and the mountains, but they refused, while humankind was foolish enough to accept it. In this acceptance Talbi sees the 'tragic' dimension of human destiny. (*Comprendre* [Paris] 98, November 1970.)

For Further Reading

1. Islam

Several translations of the Qur'an into English are available. Among those by Muslims, two which both first appeared in the 1930's and have since then been widely used and frequently reprinted in different editions are: *The Meaning of the Glorious Koran*, by Mohammed Marmaduke Pickthall, and *The Holy Qur'an: Text Translation and Commentary*, by Abdullah Yusuf Ali. More recently, there is *The Qur'an: a New Translation*, by M. A. S. Abdel Haleem (Oxford University Press, 2010). Among translations by non-Muslims, *The Koran Interpreted*, by Arthur Arberry, first published in 1955 and often reprinted by Oxford University Press, is widely respected.

Jacques Jomier, *The Great Themes of the Qur'an*, London, SCM, 1997.

Abdullah Saeed, *The Qur'an: an Introduction*, Oxon, Routledge, 2008.

Muhammad Muhsin Khan, *The Translation of the Meanings of Sahih al-Bukhari*, Lahore, 1983 (one of the most significant collections of hadith).

Jonathan A. C. Brown, *Hadith: Muhammad's Legacy in the Medieval and Modern World,* London, Oneworld, 2009.

Martin Lings, *Muhammad: His Life Based on the Earliest Sources*, London, Unwin Paperbacks, 1986.

Maxime Rodinson, *Muhammad* (new edition), Penguin, 1999.

Seyyed Hossein Nasr, *Ideals and Realities of Islam* (2nd edition), Aquarian Press, 1994.

Jonathan A. C. Brown, *Muhammad: a Very Short Introduction,* New York, Oxford University Press, 2011.

143

Fazlur Rahman, *Islam* (2nd edition), Chicago, Chicago University Press, 1979.

David Waines, *An Introduction to Islam* (2nd edition), New York, Cambridge University Press, 2003.

Sayyid Abul A'la Mawdudi, *Towards Understanding Islam*, Leicester, Islamic Foundation.

Hammudah Abdalati, *Islam in Focus*, Leicester, Islamic Foundation.

Annemarie Schimmel, *Mystical Dimensions of Islam*, Chapel Hill, NC, University of North Carolina Press, 1975.

Tariq Ramadan, *Radical Reform: Islamic Ethics and Liberation,* New York, Oxford University Press, 2009.

John Esposito, *The Oxford Dictionary of Islam*, New York, Oxford University Press, 2003.

2. Christianity

The New Jerusalem Bible: Standard Edition. New York, Doubleday, 1999.

Vatican Council II. *The Conciliar and Post Conciliar Documents.* Ed. Austin Flannery, O.P. New Revised Edition. New York, Costello, 1992.

J. Neuner, S.J. – J. Dupuis, S.J., *The Christian Faith in the Doctrinal Documents of the Catholic Church.* New York, Alba House, 1995.

Catechism of the Catholic Church. Second Edition. New York, Doubleday Books, 2003.

The Essential Catholic Handbook. A Summary of Beliefs, Practices and Prayers with a Glossary of Key Terms. Liguori, MO, Ligouri Publications, 2005.

Credo. A Catholic Catechism. London, G. Chapman, 1983.

Benedict XVI (Card. Joseph Ratzinger), *Introduction to Christianity*, San Francisco, Ignatius Press, 2004.

Benedict XVI (Card. Joseph Ratzinger), *Truth and Tolerance: Christian Belief and World Religions.* San Francisco, Ignatius Press, 2004.

Benedict XVI (Card. Joseph Ratzinger), *Called to Communion: Understanding the Church Today.* San Francisco, Ignatius Press, 1996.

Benedict XVI (Card. Joseph Ratzinger), *Many Religions – One Covenant: Israel, the Church and the World*, San Francisco, Ignatius Press, 1999.

Raymond E. Brown, *Responses to 101 Questions on the Bible*, Mahwah, NJ, Paulist Press, 1990.

Kallistos Ware, *The Orthodox Way*, New York, St. Vladimir's Seminary Press, 1995.

John Binns, *An Introduction to the Christian Orthodox Churches*, New York, Cambridge University Press, 2002.

Alister McGrath, *Christian Theology: an Introduction* (3rd edition), Oxford, Blackwell, 2001.

Karl Barth, *Dogmatics in Outline*, London, SCM, 1949.

Jürgen Moltmann, *The Crucified God*, London, SCM, 1974.

N. T. Wright, *The Resurrection of the Son of God*, London, SPCK, 2003.

Richard B. Hays, *The Moral Vision of the New Testament*, Edinburgh, T&T Clark, 1996.

Jacques Dupuis, *Toward a Christian Theology of Religious Pluralism*, New York, Orbis Books, 2001.

Lesslie Newbigin, *The Gospel in a Pluralist Society*, London, SPCK, 1989.

Richard Bauckham, *Jesus and the Eyewitnesses,* Grand Rapids, MI, Eerdmanns Publishing Company, 2006.

David Bentley Hart, *Atheist Delusions: The Christian Revolution and Its Fashionable Enemies,* New Haven, CT, Yale University Press, 2009.

3. Christian-Muslim Dialogue

Kenneth Cragg, *The Call of the Minaret* (revised edition), London, Oneworld, 2000.

Ismail Raji al-Faruqi, *Islam and Other Faiths* (ed. Ataullah Siddiqui), Leicester, Islamic Foundation.

Kate Zebiri, *Muslims and Christians Face to Face*, London, Oneworld, 1997.

Badru D Kateregga and David W Shenk, *Islam and Christianity: a Muslim and a Christian in Dialogue*, Nairobi, 1980.

Glory E. Dharmaraj and Jacob S. Dharmaraj, *Christianity and Islam: a Missiological Encounter*, Delhi, ISPCK, 1999.

Khurshid Ahmad and David Kerr (eds.), *Christian Mission and Islamic Da'wah*, Leicester, The Islamic Foundation, 1982.

Sidney H. Griffith, *The Church in the Shadow of the Mosque,* Princeton, NJ, Princeton University Press, 2008.

Christian W. Troll, *Dialogue and Difference: Clarity in Christian-Muslim Relations,* New York: Orbis, 2010.

The following websites provide information about some ongoing approaches to Christian-Muslim dialogue:

A Common Word: http://www.acommonword.com/.
Building Bridges: http://berkleycenter.georgetown.edu/resources/networks/building_bridges.
Scriptural Reasoning: http://etext.lib.virginia.edu/journals/jsrforum/.
Answers to Muslims online: http://www.answers-to-muslims.com.